Praise for *It's for the Horses*

"To teach is my responsibility.
To watch those taught grow, is my reward."
~ Diane J. Sept

There is a beauty when two individuals are in honor of each other's being.

The peace that is created when each partner understands and appreciates the other's offering is a time of undeniable appreciation.

Dutch Henry finds joy as he guides the horse/human relationship closer to and into this space.

This project compiles Dutch Henry's years of experience gathering helpful—sometimes life-altering—exercises for the horse. This ability to help the horse sometimes reciprocates in a life-altering shift in the human.

Dutch has found and follows the guidance of horse professionals who honor that which he honors. These exercises are based on the truth of the whole horse—emotional, mental, physical.

Enjoy the wonderful way of Dutch Henry's writing. Enjoy soaking in this supportive way with your horse. Enjoy the shift in you and your horse's relationship.

Thank you, Dutch Henry.

~ **Diane J. Sept**,
   Connected Riding Senior instructor and
   owner of Back To Basics Equine Awareness

For many, horses today are viewed more as companions or members of the family rather than beasts of burden. Although the concept of natural care and handling has grown by leaps and bounds this past decade, there still are instances where humans, either because of lack of knowledge or just not caring, still do injustice to the equines in their life. Thankfully, Dutch Henry has made it his life's passion to be an advocate of the horse through educating people in all aspects of horse care.

In this book, *It's for the Horses*, Dutch covers what we can do to become better guardians for our equines by understanding their needs, truly encompassing mind, body and soul. I think that if horses could write, they would have compiled a book like this!

It's for the Horses is a passionate, highly useful resource for all people who want to do right by the equines in their life. This book belongs in every horse person's library, but best kept within close reach as it is a book to be referred back to often.

Thank you, Dutch!

~ **Lisa Ross-Williams**,
Publisher/Editor-In-Chief, Natural Horse Magazine and author of the award-winning book, Down-To-Earth Natural Horse Care.

It's not easy changing the world. Especially when it usually means effecting a shift in perspective.

The dreaded "C" word... change.

So when you find someone else who believes as strongly in the need for this change as you do, and is working as hard at it as you yourself are doing, then a kinship will almost always evolve. I believe that things would immediately improve for every horse on this planet if we could effect one simple little change, one tiny little shift in perspective.

Dutch Henry believes this as well and that is why I so strongly recommend his latest book,

It's for the Horses. Because if we could convince every horse owner on the planet to make every decision about their horses from the perspective of the horse, not from the perspective of the owner—from the horse's end of the lead rope—then everything would change immediately. Relationship, training and the health and happiness of the horse. Kathleen and I have proven it. Dutch Henry has proven it. And everything he has written in

It's for the Horses will lift you closer and closer to those goals. And closer and closer to your horses.

Read it. You will not regret it. Nor will your horses.

Thank you for this, Dutch Henry.

~ Joe Camp, author of the national best-seller,
The Soul of a Horse—Life Lessons from the Herd
and its Amazon #1 best-selling sequel
Born Wild—The Soul of a Horse

Also By Dutch Henry:

We'll Have The Summer
Tom Named By Horse

It's for the Horses

An advocate's musings about their needs, spirit, gifts and care

By Dutch Henry

For my wife, daughter and grandchildren,
with love.

And, for the horses.

ACKNOWLEDGEMENTS

All the horses I've had the privilege and honor of
knowing who have taught me to understand and see
things from their perspective.

My mentor, Diane Sept, who gave me the tools
I needed to learn from those horses.

Peggy Cummings, Linda Tellington-Jones and
many others who gave me valuable lessons as my
journey to help horses continued.

My wife Robin, who supported my quest with
love, understanding and patience—And took the
wonderful cover photo.

Our Coffee Clutch blog followers and
Facebook friends who requested I put my blog posts
in a book.

Bobbie Jo Lieberman,
Editor of trailBLAZER magazine who worked
her editing magic. Bobbie can be contacted at
spiritofgypsy@gmail.com

My friend Oz Dillon for taking the photographs.
Oz Dillon (Odee) is on Facebook

Troy Locker Palmer of PhGroup
for a great cover, and layout and design. Troy can
be reached by email at troy@phgindustries.com
and visit her website www.phgindustries.com.

Thank you all.

Before we start,
a few thoughts from Dutch Henry

Howdy Friends!

There are barns full of how-to books for horse lovers, owners and caregivers out there. Do we really need another one? I don't know if we do, but I believe your horses will be happy if you have a look at this one.

Quite simply, I'm a horse advocate. Everything I do is from the horse's perspective, including this little book. Every story, idea, suggestion and thought on these pages will be to suggest and share thoughts and ideas on how to maximize a relationship between horse and human—from the horse's point of view.

Having had the honor and privilege of working for a number of years rehabilitating Tennessee Walking Horses with my mentor Diane Sept, a Senior Certified Connected Riding® Instructor, I learned from her, and the horses, many things. Among them I learned the techniques of Peggy Cummings' Connected Riding and Groundwork® and Linda Tellington-Jones' Tellington TTouch®. Within the coming pages, I will often reference Peggy and Linda and their techniques, and I highly recommend you purchase their books and DVDs. You'll find their contacts in the Resources and References section near the end of this book.

Often I'll mention Diane Sept. I always say, "Everything good I know about horses I learned from Diane. Everything good I know about life I learned from my wife." From Diane I learned patience, how to truly hear a horse. How to understand a horse. Of course the horses taught me much too, but Diane taught me how to be a better student. Thank you Diane for all you've done, and do, for the horses.

For some time now, I've had the privilege of writing for several equine publications. I've had columns in TrailBLAZER and Natural Horse magazines. Writing for these and other wonderful publications, I've been lucky to interview and write stories about, and learn from, some mighty fine people. Each of them has left their imprint on me. Each of them has helped me understand more.

Over the years, I've met and worked with horses who taught me many things: their emotions, their joys, their sadness and their spirit. Including the big horses on the farm I had been dumped off on as a child, discarded like an unwanted cat. As I sat huddled in the corner of their stall, today nearly half a century later, I remember that moment as the first time I ever felt safe. I didn't know it then, but that was the first time I'd ever felt the spirit of the horse. Often I have felt that spirit in horses touch me, guide me and even ask me questions.

This is not a book about riding or training horses. This is a book on my thoughts, ideas and suggestions on how folks might find the joy in doing things for the horse, with the horse's point of view as the leading guide. It is my hope to help as many people as possible learn to hear the horse, feel their spirit, and in that way help horses everywhere.

This book is a compilation of my Coffee Clutch blog posts from the past few years, thank you Coffee Clutch followers for the request. I've kept in place my original blog-style format, so each story has a "Howdy" and my signature, "GittyUp," which I fondly adopted from my biggest hero, Winnie the Pooh. I also kept intact the homespun, conversational style used in my Coffee Clutch blog because we are having friendly chats together. You'll meet my wonderful wife, the Ravishin' Robbie. You'll meet my mare Kessy, our cats Miss Kitty and Tigger, our dog Saturday, all of whom join Kessy and me for our morning Coffee Clutch—coffee in the barn each morning, which gave birth to our Coffee Clutch blog. Above all, I hope in these pages and chats you can find things to take with you to enrich your relationship with your horses, and all horses. Because never forget, "It's for the Horses."

Gitty Up ~ *Dutch Henry*

THE COFFEE CLUTCH BUNCH.

It's not really a barn, just a three-sided run-in where Kessy, Saturday the dog, the cats, chickens and I greet every day.

I would love to hear from you.
My email is dutchhenry@hughes.net
You can also find me on Facebook, and
my Coffee Clutch blog – dutchhenry.blogspot.com

Table of Contents

SECTION III — Understanding Your Horse

SECTION IV — Building Trust and Confidence

SECTION V—Horse Care

SECTION VI—Horsemanship

SECTION VII—Those Who Shaped Me

FOREWORD

By Bobbie Jo Lieberman

Editor-in-Chief, trailBLAZER magazine

Dutch Henry is on a mission to help people see their horses with new eyes, to listen with new ears, to touch their lives with greater sensitivity and awareness. How many of us take the time to truly listen to our horses? To pay attention to what they are trying to tell us? Instead, we are often advised to "Show him who's boss," and "Don't let her get away with it." Dutch doesn't buy into this paradigm, which is dominance by any other name. Instead, he is here to show us a kinder, gentler way to win the respect and, yes—the love—of our horses in a non-coercive, non-threatening, non-intimidating way.

Dutch has had some terrific teachers. His mentor for the last 20 years was (and is) Dianne Sept, a student of both Linda Tellington-Jones and Peggy Cummings. Dutch's work stands strongly on the shoulders of these pioneers of the horse world. He has integrated their work into a program that can help your horse progress quickly, without fear or force. One of his most powerful reminders for us is to "Ignore the negative, celebrate the positive." Take your attention away from whether your horse did what you wanted. If he didn't, just ask again, or ask in another way. When your horse responds, praise him to the moon with kind words and a soft touch.

Ever wonder why, when you send a horse out for "training," the horse comes home... and is still herd-bound, buddy-sour or (name that behavior)? In the words of Tellington-Jones, "A horse trained by force will test every new rider." Tellington-Jones, Peggy Cummings and Dianne Sept were the forerunners who inspired Dutch Henry on his journey to understanding our equine friends. A journey that led to many insights into how we can better relate to them and ultimately develop the mutual trust and unshakeable bond we all dream of having with our horses.

The illustrated groundwork exercises within this book can help any horse become safer, calmer and more willing. Just a few minutes a day, or at least each time you ride, can make all the difference! If every rider would simply ask her horse to "Rock Back" as she prepares to ride, and do the "One-Step" forward and "One-Step" back exercise with diagonal pairs of legs, the difference will be clear and immediate, as the horse shifts her weight off the forehand. As you will see, this makes things so much easier for the horse. It will also give you great insights into your horse's flexibility, balance and posture.

As Dutch says, "This is not a book about riding or training horses. This is a book on my thoughts, ideas and suggestions on how folks might find the joy in doing things for the horse, with the horse's point of view as the leading guide. It is my hope to help as many people as possible learn to hear the horse, feel their spirit, and in that way help horses everywhere."

It has often been said that our horses are our greatest teachers. Dutch Henry, who has opened his heart, mind and soul to the horse, is living proof of that statement.

Enjoy the learning as we join Dutch on a remarkable journey.

My Tribute to Horses
Horses Among Us, Thank God

Howdy Friends,

It is often said that throughout history, everywhere man has gone he has been carried upon the back of a noble horse. They've plowed our fields, carried us into and died with us in our wars, pulled our wagons and travois laden with treasured possessions to new lands and pulled our wedding carriages. They've run our races, herded our cattle, given explosive demonstrations of their power and agility in rodeos. They've strutted their magnificence in arenas before cheering crowds to win ribbons unimportant to them. When I think of the horse's spirit and how it has selflessly carried the spirit of man through the ages, I'm awed at the nobility of them. How they have answered every call with strength, beauty and unquestioning devotion. No matter the sacrifice. Today, the noble horse is embarking on perhaps his most important calling ... the healing of man.

Being a writer and horse advocate, I've had the privilege of writing hundreds of stories about what I call "People and Horses Helping Horses and People." I've met unbelievably self-sacrificing people who mortgage their homes to keep the doors open so children dealing with Autism, Down Syndrome and other unkind conditions can learn to smile and even laugh while being carried away to a happy place on the back of a therapy horse. I've met Veterans who've conquered the stranglehold of PTSD while holding the reins. I've met battered women who've learned to love and trust again simply sitting in a stall with a quiet horse. And I've met many understanding, care-giving therapy horses. I've met women and men who devote their lives to protecting our wild horses, struggling with them to allow the wild horses to remain free to run.

What lives there in the spirit of the horse that touches so many human spirits? Heals so many hearts? Builds so much courage in souls who need that courage? Offers so much exhilaration wrapped in a bundle of giving? What lives there? I propose it is simply the very spirit of the horses themselves. Horses are made that way. Why does that spirit touch man so easily? Is it simplistic to say, but is it because they can? Because they understand they should?

For centuries, the noble horse was viewed as a tool—a servant, even a weapon. Patiently they've endured all manner of servitude while waiting for mankind to learn to understand they were much more than that. We now live in a more enlightened age, where it is finally becoming not only fun but also correct to see things from the horse's perspective.

Of course, over the centuries there have been individuals who promoted the wellbeing of the horse, and history records some of their early efforts. The ancient Greek Xenophon (c. 430-354 BC) may have been the earliest human ever to promote sympathetic training and humane treatment for horses. Did you know the ancient Greeks did not shoe their horses, and it was Xenophon who first pointed out that "naturally sound hooves get spoiled in most stalls," and in his classic work "On Horsemanship" advised measures to strengthen horses' feet? Both Xenophon and Hippocrates (c. 460-370 BC) wrote of the mind and health benefits of horseback riding.

Why do I say the noble horse is perhaps embarking on his most important calling yet, "the healing of man?" As I interviewed and wrote the stories of equine-assisted therapy centers, it was both wonderful and surprising to see the sudden increase of centers for healing through horses dealing with emotional stress and pain. Originally, equine-assisted therapy had primarily focused on physical healing therapy. But in recent years more and more centers are being opened to deal with psychological and emotional trauma. Is it possible that as society races headlong into the "technology age" and moving farther and farther away from nature, we are experiencing a shift in our roots that creates a new kind of stress? A kind of stress borne of too much too fast?

I believe that horses have the ability to "slow us down while lifting us up." To help us focus within and be better for it. Most everyone in the horse world is familiar with Winston Churchill's famous quote, "There is something about the outside of a horse that is good for the inside of a man." Churchill also said, "No hour of life is wasted that is spent in the saddle." Oliver Wendell Holmes said, "To many the words, love, hope and dreams are synonymous with horse." Herman Melville told us, "Honor lies in the mane of a horse."

The Bedouins believe "The horse is a gift from God." And that "The wind of heaven is that which blows between a horse's ears." So precious to the Bedouins were their horses that many shared their master's tent. The young boys of the great Lakota Sioux Nation were assigned the job of watching and caring for the horses so that they may grow up understanding them. Touching their spirit. The Lakota understood the spirit in many things.

The spirit of the horse is patient. It is willing and powerful. And most important of all, it is healing. Over the centuries, the horse has been ever willing to be our servant and our confidant. Our healer. History is filled with stories of lives changed forever and even saved by horses.

The road has not been an easy one for the noble horse. It seems each century brings with it a new set of demands, obligations and even suffering at the hands of their human partners. And yet the noble horse stands vigilant, ever at the ready to carry us, to heal us.

Even in this age of enlightenment, many horses still suffer at the hand of harsh trainers, owners and circumstances, and it is difficult to understand how, still today, so many people can put their own interests, pursuits and wealth above the horse's well being. A friend once told me, "When horses and money compete, horses loose." Perhaps one day, the spirit of the horse can touch so many that these practices will forever become a thing of the past.

Some people suggest that to project our human emotions onto the horse is folly. I proclaim to not do so is, in fact, the biggest folly of all. If you've ever watched a mare scream for her foal as they are yanked apart on a Bureau of Land Management roundup, you know of their emotions. If you've ever watched a horse tread lightly while carrying the precious cargo of a therapeutic rider, you know their emotions.

As more and more people learn to understand and even feel the spirit of the horse in this enlightened age we find ourselves in, the noble horse is here to once again carry our burden. Even if this time the burden is more emotional than physical. Trainers are more and more willing to "see and teach from the horse's perspective." More and more students are being taught to consider what the benefit to the horse might be as together they pursue mastering skills in the ring, on the trail and on the course. More and more young people are becoming horse enthusiasts because they can not only learn new skills and have fun, but they can help others too.

The rise in the number of equine-assisted therapy centers offers wonderful opportunities for folks who have no way of owning a horse of their own to feel the love, spirit and emotions of the horse by volunteering at a local center. The therapy horses at those centers not only help those receiving the therapy but those volunteering, too. Volunteers who otherwise would never know the connection between human and horse can feel the connection to nature in today's busy digital world. Many times, the horses who give so much love at these centers are in fact horses who have been rescued themselves. They may have spent time at a rescue where volunteers have the joy of getting to feel their spirit and learn from them. Even as the horses are being rehabilitated themselves, they are able and willing to teach. To show hurried individuals the value and healing powers of slowing down to horse time.

Trainers and clinicians teaching the natural way while considering the horse's perspective are becoming more numerous today and attracting large followings. More and more people are finding their way back to nature under the tutelage of a skilled instructor and an understanding horse. Do we have more to learn from this great gift from God, the horse? I submit yes. And, I also promise the horse will be there to teach us.

Gitty Up ~ *Dutch Henry*

SECTION 1

Hearing Your Horse

I've chosen to start with a section on hearing your horse because it is the very foundation of everything you'll do with your horse, any horse. You'll find my thoughts and stories here with helpful tips and ways to increase your reception, communication and connection.

Spirituality and Horses...and Us

—————⟨✵⟩—————

Howdy Friends,

Anyone who ever sat with a horse alone in a barn, walked a trail among nature's beauty with a horse, or hugged a horse's neck while crying out tears of sad, happy or worry, has felt the spirit of the horse connect to their heart. I was about 10, sitting with the horses one of the first nights on the farm I'd been dumped off on like a stray cat. I didn't have any tears, hope or dreams left, but I remember it was the first time in my young life I'd ever felt safe, welcome. I didn't know it then, but it was the first time I'd felt the spirit of the horse.

It would be nearly half a century later while Reiki Master Maxine Hollinger was helping me that together we discovered my spirit guides are horses. It was an extraordinary moment, though deep inside perhaps not a total surprise.

I've long said horses and humans have a spiritual connection on a level so different than any other. Of course dogs and cats and many animals have connections that are wonderful, but horses, if we let them, will touch and guide us in ways that connect to our spirit, our soul and our heart.

As I said in my tribute to horses, "When I think of the horse's spirit and how he has selflessly carried the spirit of man through the ages, I'm awed at the nobility of them. How they have answered every call with strength, beauty and unquestioning devotion. No matter the sacrifice. Today, the noble horse is embarking on perhaps his most important calling … the healing of man." It is with that tremendous spirit they will selflessly heal us, make us better beings. It is out there for all to see in the explosion of equine-assisted therapy programs and centers throughout the world.

If we listen, our horses will teach us about patience, kindness and humbleness. They'll introduce us to beauty, connection and responsibility.

Even as tens of thousands of wild horses endure the unkind, ignorant hand of man in BLM holding pens, in torture barns of the Tennessee Walking Horse "big lick" insanity and as other breeds suffer the heavy hand of man's misguided pursuit of fame, money and who knows what. They wait patiently to teach us, heal us.

Their spirit is calling us to understand there are things greater than money, fame and ourselves. Riding my mare Kessy alone through the forest, she'll often stop and take a long soulful look into the trees. She's not always looking at anything in particular. I hear her telling me, "Take a moment to enjoy this."

Isn't that a beautiful sentiment? Spirits connect, minds and hearts come together. I see it all the time at equine-assisted therapy events when the magic touches the hearts and spirits of folks. They may not have totally understood, but they've felt the spirit of the horse.

Is there a spiritual connection between human and horse? You bet there is, and thank God for it.

Gitty Up ~ *Dutch Henry*

And So It Grows

Howdy Friends,

And so it grows. Isn't that a beautiful thought? I was writing to a friend last evening about all the things she taught me that I have shared with others who have in turn then shared that knowledge with still more folks. That's what we do, isn't it? Share the good we learn.

Each time I write about birds, bird watching, wildflowers or butterflies, I think of all the people who have taught me so much. Some of those dear friends are gone now, but their wisdom and knowledge goes on because we share it with each other. Funny how certain birds will make me remember friends who the loved that bird. Our friend Annabelle, who we often talk about in the Coffee Clutch, is now in a nursing home but still insists I call her weekly with my birding results. She loves all the birds and her Cardinals best. Pat, now gone, loved her Bluebirds. As do I. She taught me so much over the years. Sharing what she taught me about Bluebirds and many others, and wildflowers too, keeps her memory alive. And keeps the knowledge growing in wider circles.

My mentor, Diane Sept, taught me so much about horses, their health, their spirit, their ability to love, teach and heal. Their ability to talk with us, if we listen we can hear them. Each time I work with horses, my own, or horses in my "Therapy For Therapy Horses" clinics I think of her. I marvel at how she can be helping those horses and their people without ever meeting them. Her wisdom, teachings and helping reaches out through me, and the folks to whom I introduce her techniques to make their lives better. It's like ripples in a pond spreading out farther and farther. How many horses has Diane helped by teaching me? And in turn my showing others, who then pass that knowledge on. The horses, too, I've met who have taught me so much that can be shared, and passed on. And so it grows.

When I think of all the good things about life I learned from my dear wife, Robbie, I can only hope to be as giving and patient as she, and pass on what she taught me about caring for, and understanding others, first. When we teach our children and grandchildren, and they grow into adulthood and in turn teach their own children things they learned from us, about life, love and sharing the good. And so it grows.

So as you go along, give a thought every now and then to those who inspired you to become who you are, and how they, through you, are inspiring others they may never meet. That's a beautiful thing.

Share also the wisdom horses have given you, because you listened. And so it grows.

Gitty Up ~ *Dutch Henry*

Are You Listening?

Howdy Friends,

Finally the rain started. We'd been gathered in Kessy's barn for half an hour already, Kessy, Tigger, Saturday, Miss Kitty and me watching the clouds thicken. I was on my second cup of Folgers. A few chickens wandered in and out. The hummingbird feeder was busy, too, much ado about nectar. A train rumbled in the distance, its whistle blew as it crossed a road somewhere far from our cozy Coffee Clutch. Deep in the woods a Cardinal sang his fluted song. When the skies opened the sudden pounding on the tin startled Kessy, she snapped up her head, marched to the door and with her head high, investigated the dark clouds. Satisfied all was well, she carefully stepped backward to her hay, shoved her nose deep into the soft pale green pile and munched away.

I had an interesting talk with some friends over the weekend about riding, horses and life. For me, my thoughts are always guided by Robbie, Love and Horses. And Nature. It's funny, though, how my analogies and opinions most always have some reference to horses. Horses like it when you give them the time they need to make sense of something you're asking them to do. So do people, and children. Horses like us to lead by example. So do people, and children. Horses blossom best when you ignore the negative and celebrate the positive. So do people, and children.

It seems like today folks are a bit too quick to point out the negatives and shortcomings of other folks, their children and even spouses. I have a hard time listening to all that ... And I sure find it challenging to hear folks complain about their horse. "He won't do this or that … He's stupid … He's not listening to me!" Sometimes I hold my tongue. Sometimes I ask, "Are you listening?"

Have a great day today! Maybe take a few minutes and listen. You might be surprised at what you learn, if you listen long enough.

Gitty Up ~ *Dutch Henry*

Listening Not Whispering

Howdy Friends,

I sat in the car waiting as I often do while Ravishin' Robbie ran into the store to grab a few groceries. It's not so much I don't enjoy shopping, but walking in stores is a bother to my legs. And it offers a great time to people-watch. The other day I was "people watchin'" when I noticed a child of, I suppose 7 or so, trying oh-so-hard to get her mother's understanding of a matter of what must have been great importance by the demonstration of arm flailing and hurried loud outbursts. Of course I couldn't understand the words, but the volume and tone sent a clear, "Are You Listening?" I chuckled because I knew the answer was a resounding NO! For the mother was every bit as determined to make her point at the same time.

I never got the impression they were angry—quite the opposite, they seemed happy and excited, but were not able to communicate whatever was so exciting.

This made me think of a seminar I went to for sales training years ago, "Learning effective ways to listen." Never forgot it. But I must admit I'm not that great a listener, either. Unless I use this little trick. And you bet, I'm gonna share how I modified it for listening to your horse.

The trick isn't to watch the other person's lips or focus on their eyes or get in sync with their breathing, or any of the standard "rules for good listening." In fact you can do this with your eyes closed. Well with people you can. With horses you pretty much gotta look at them.

But with people it is really simple. Here it is: "Listen to every word as if you must jump in and finish the sentence." That's it ... No gimmicks, no tricks. Just pretend at any moment you'll need to pick it up and finish the sentence. We even did role-playing in the seminar, which I remember was a hoot!

So how do you finish the sentence your horse is saying? Well you listen closely, it will enrich your connection. A brief side note here: When I'm doing my "Therapy For Therapy Horses" exercises, within a few moments of starting, I'll get signals from the horse where they want my hands to go next. It is one reason why I'd love for anyone who has or works with horses to learn at least the basics of these. These exercises will teach folks to "listen to their horse" in a most comprehensive way.

But I'd like to share the other way you can finish your horse's sentence. Think about when you're leading her, and she stops. I'd like to suggest that you stop too. Don't just think what you want, where you are going or want to go, but pause a second or three and look where your horse is looking. Sometimes it's obvious, she's worried about something she sees, with ears and eyes focused right on it. That's an easy one and you should look at it too and wait a few seconds before asking her to move on. Finish the sentence together.

The real opportunity to finish your horse's sentence will come when she stops as you're leading her, you turn to look at her ... and she isn't really looking at anything. She's just standing with soft eyes, relaxed ears and no concern on her face. This is your chance to hear her, and finish her sentence. If you stay soft, open your heart, mind and intuitiveness, you'll pick up on it. It'll be a moment of deep connection. Think then of the end of her sentence ... Will she walk on to follow you, or relax another moment? Think a bit, wait for it, and then you'll see, your thoughts were in tune. You heard her—because you were listening ... and the opposite is also true. If when she stops, you tug on the lead to move her on with no more than a brief glance her way shouting in your mind, "Come On!" You will have missed what she was trying to tell you when she said, "I'm really loving this walk together."

I'm a big fan of groundwork with horses. Doing slow easy things together will give you many opportunities to finish your horse's sentences. Remember to pause, join her thoughts and "predict" what she wants to do next, by finishing her sentence. While trail riding is another great chance to "learn to listen well," if she stops along the trail, pause, look and listen to her. The key to listening well is finishing the sentence in the way the "talker" would finish it. You know then you are in tune.

Happy listening!

Gitty Up ~ *Dutch Henry*

Let Your Horse Slow You Down

---❖---

Howdy Friends,

In your busy life, let your horse slow you down. They'll do it, if you listen. They have many subtle, and sometimes not so subtle, ways of cutting through the fog of hurry-up-go-mode to help us focus on the moment. To see the world as it can be seen. The glory and beauty of it. The peacefulness and rewards it can offer us, if we slow down and process the moment.

Our Coffee Clutch family knows I start each day in the barn enjoying the finest brew Folgers decaf has to offer (I'm a connoisseur of fine coffee blends) and the quiet company of my mare Kessy as well as Saturday, our cats, Tigger, Miss Kitty, Lil' Bit, Fluffernutter, Daniel Striped Tiger and Bullet. It's a time of gentle reflection and absorption of goodness, peace and sometimes reflection. I watch the birds at the feeders and chicken scratching, listen to Saturday snore, Kitty purr and Kessy munch her hay. I thank God each morning for a beautiful day—sun, rain, wind or snow—they're all beautiful. The anchor of our morning meditation is Kessy. Her spirit welcomes us to live in the moment with no worries or anxieties. Sure, not everyone has an hour or so to spend just sitting with their horse in the morning. But what if you had 10 minutes, sometime each day when you could sit with your horse and slow down your thoughts? Try it; you'll feel the slowing. Your horse will feel it too.

When your horse stops to snare a nibble of grass as you ride along and you ask her to walk on, pause and wait. Many times a horse will happily walk on, after they grab two or three more mouthfuls. If we yank on the reins, kick and demand, they'll probably still grab those extra mouthfuls, but you're teaching her resistance, rather than allowing her to teach you, to slow down and enjoy the moment. So in this case simply ask her to walk on with a kiss or cluck, and perhaps a gentle heel touch, and wait. When she takes that extra bite, she'll raise her head and walk on softly. If she knows she can rely on your patience, you can rely on her harmony.

In fact, whenever you ask something of your horse, allow the pause. It's for you, more than the horse. We humans are too often wired to go quickly. Instant results. How many times have you seen and heard friends say, "Whoa, whoa, whoa?" when one "whoa" is all that's really required? And preferred by horses. Asking once, allowing the pause, and then seeing the result will slow you down, and in the long run, shorten the time needed for response. You'll both be softer, more in the moment. And because you're in the moment, in tune with your horse, you'll see, feel and hear your horse on an all-new level. True harmony.

So if you haven't already, go ahead, let your horse slow you down.

Gitty Up ~ *Dutch Henry*

Listening to Your Horse Pt 1

———⟨✴⟩———

Howdy Friends,

Listening to your horse. I know that may sometimes be easy to say, but difficult to actually do. Sometimes we listen and try to understand, but we have a hard time getting and perhaps understanding the messages. I'm one who believes it is a lot better to "listen" than "whisper." Somebody asked me about that one time and I said, "You can't listen if you're whispering."

A Coffee Clutch friend emailed me about my "Therapy For Therapy Horses" clinics to ask about horses with old injuries and if the exercises could be modified to accommodate the injuries. That's what put the "listening" thing in my head this morning.

I truly believe the exercises I incorporated into my "Therapy For Therapy Horses" clinics not only help the horse feel better, relax and release, as well as become much more attentive, willing and eager, but doing these exercises for and with your horse will fine tune your own listening skills.

As you do these exercises, it is important to "feel" the horse. "Hear" the horse. Because, for instance as you lightly "Wiggle the Poll," you're waiting for the release response of dropping the head, or softening the neck, or taking a deep breath as if to say, "Ahh, Thank You." Or the opposite may occur. The horse may raise her head in protest as if to say, "No, you may not touch me there!" That's a conversation. If you're listening, you then know you'll need to begin with the "Poll Wiggle" farther down the neck, closer to the withers. This horse worries about being touched at the poll or on the ears area. This is an easy one to understand and "Hear." But as you continue with other exercises, your ability to hear your horse and comprehend what she is telling you will sharpen.

NOTE – To see photos of these exercises, please go to the Exercises To Help Your Horse ... and You section where you'll find these and other exercises described with photos.

Yes you can do these exercises with and for any horse, even, especially, work through injuries. Start with exercises in areas that are not related to any of the injuries and teach your horse the feeling of relaxing and releasing there. At the same time you will be learning to "Listen" to your horse and follow the cues she is giving you as to how much she can and wants to do. As you master the ability to "Hear" your horse you can move gradually into the areas affected by the injuries. You may need to modify the technique a bit, but by now, your horse will guide you.

As you do each of these exercises, you will receive messages from your horse communicating either "This is wonderful" or "I do not understand this" or "I need you to take this slower," for instance. But as you and you horse go along, your communicating skills will improve greatly, and one of the wonderful things about these exercises is this newfound ability to hear each other will be carried over to whatever you do together. Trail ride, barrel race, hunter/jumper— whatever your discipline, however you play together, your level of understanding, listening to and giving cues to each other will become a fine-tuned art. These exercises "Give back to the horse" for sure, but they "Give back to you" too.

And as you learn to "Listen" to your horse, you'll be amazed at how much information is in an unbalanced or a balanced stance, or a half-closed eye, or a dropped hip. As your horse teaches you to "Hear" her ... She might also be teaching you to hear people, too.

Gitty Up ~ *Dutch Henry*

Listening to Your Horse Pt 2

———⟨✷⟩———

Howdy Friends,

Last evening I conducted my first ever over-the-phone "Therapy For Therapy Horses" clinic. A Facebook friend had emailed me with questions about modifying the exercises for horses with old injuries. Oh we had a wonderful chat. She is an accomplished horsewoman and her horses have a terrific mommy who showers them with tons of love. She has a Quarter Horse who has a broken tail and a Thoroughbred who suffered a bad stifle injury, which left him a bit off and with issues in his sacral area.

I'm sharing a bit about our chat, because it is a great example to talk about these exercises. Since these exercises are totally non-invasive and are soft and gentle, and are in fact all about helping the horse learn to "heal himself," they are perfect to use safely on horses with a few squeaky joints. Just start in areas that are not affected by the injury, so you'll learn to "hear" the signals your horses sends as to how she likes or worries about the exercise and the feel of release, worry or satisfaction.

In our "phone clinic" I first had to devise a perfect way to describe the "touch," or amount of pressure used for, the poll wiggle, vertebrae wiggle and other exercises, I usually actually demonstrate the range of wiggle and pressure by wiggling the person's shoulder, and by doing that the participants are always shocked at how far down their body they can feel the release. It is exactly the release the horse feels on the "poll wiggle" that travels back through their spine. After we mastered describing touch and wiggle, things went swimmingly. Now understanding that feel, and having a full grasp of the vertebrae wiggle, which goes all the way to the tip of the tail, our friend can work up to giving her Quarter Horse a try at the "tail pull," which was one of her big concerns. It will be a modified tail pull, but I'm confident it'll be great. NOTE – To see photos of these exercises, please go to the Exercises To Help Your Horse ... and You section where you'll find these and other exercises described with photos.

I also talked her through the "hip wiggle," for her horse with the sacral and stifle issue, which will really help free up and strengthen those areas giving him better range of motion and a lot of relief.

The totally wonderful thing about these exercises is how easy they are to learn and how much good they will do for your horse, and you. Even with horses who have physical conditions, injuries or problems that are life long, these exercises can help them regain so much correct and comfortable body carriage, relief and confidence that the old problems will greatly improve. And as you work with them your ability to understand and "hear" your horse will grow and grow. Your relationship will reach levels you never might have imagined. You'll truly begin to hear each other on a level you might not have known existed. Your horse will guide you as you learn to truly, listen. The listening skills your horse will teach you will transfer to many other areas of life, too.

So, since we've figured out how to conduct "Therapy For Therapy Horses" clinics over the phone, if you have questions you'd like to ask, please email me, we can exchange phone numbers and do remote clinics. It's all about "helping the horses."

dutchhenry@hughes.net

Gitty Up ~ *Dutch Henry*

Listening to Your Horse Pt 3
Misunderstanding

—————⟨✦⟩—————

Howdy Friends,

Okay I'm sorry and I promise this will be the last (for a while) about this listening thing, but stuff keeps pushing its way into my head. Like yesterday when I was giving therapy to Donnie, a stunning Paint who has had a busy career already in his young life. Donnie is 13, and like many horses, he's been around the block a few times. His first job was as a stallion, I suppose because he is so stunning. He then earned a living as a carriage horse, and now he provides physical therapy to children and doubles as a lesson horse. Donnie is a very trusting, loving and giving horse. He will do whatever is asked but internalizes everything, keeping his body rigid and hard. This is often the case with horses who want so much to please. They try so hard they may completely lose any connection with their own body.

Petey was there too yesterday. Petey is only 3. He had what I consider a rough start. His first experience in his learning to "obey" was as a colt in an operation that teaches folks how to "break" (their word, NOT mine) horses. His experience in that theater left him with issues of trust and confusion. He now worries a lot about "getting it right" and has great difficulty focusing and relaxing. While Petey has near perfect manners, he worries about himself and takes his mind away from anything the least bit challenging by fidgeting, nipping and looking far away.

I write these thoughts NOT as a trainer, for I certainly am not one, nor do I intend to hold myself out as one. But as we did our "Therapy for Therapy

Horses" exercises yesterday, I was thinking about how differently each horse "spoke," just trying to be understood. Yesterday was the 4th time I visited them, and during that time both have made terrific progress. It's so exciting to see and feel the changes in not just their body carriage but in their their attitude and conversation, too!

Donnie has begun to soften his body, which at first felt like a rock from nose to tail, and take a bit more care about how he uses his body, which has greatly reduced the tightness in his neck, chest back and hips. He has begun to lift his back higher and is no longer on his forehand. Petey, too, is much softer, and while he still worries and fears every cue, he fidgets far less, rarely nips and almost never flinches when touched. His stride has become longer and with softer foot placement.

Misunderstanding comes into to play because both these horses had a history of being "told" what to do, how to do it and never "asked." Both Donnie and Petey complied, but it took a toll on their minds and bodies. By introducing them to these simple exercises, they were allowed to relax and "talk" for themselves without the fear of being "disciplined," or a "demand" being given. Donnie's expressions are more outward and lively; Petey no longer rebels or spins at the mere "thought" of a touch. He also lowers his head, allows a hand on his poll ... and stands quietly (most of the time).

Gitty Up ~ *Dutch Henry*

Note: You will learn about these exercises and my clinics I call "Therapy For Therapy Horses Clinics" in our next section, "Exercises To Help Your Horse ... and You."

Horse Communication

———‹✿›———

Howdy Friends,

Horse communication. There are a lot of folks who truly understand it. There are a lot of folks who wish they did. There are plenty of folks who disregard it, even consider those who believe in communicating with horses or any animal silly, or worse.

The first step to communicating with your horse is simply to believe. Believe it is possible, and believe what you hear. As children we were all deeply in tune to receiving voices from animals and our intuition, but as we grow and are encouraged to disregard those thoughts as foolishness, some of us follow that wrongheaded advice. Others questioned it, and some, like me, found that animals are the most honest friends of all.

One of the most common objections I've heard over the years is "If you can talk to your horse, why can't you make her 'do whatever.'" My standard reply is "You can talk to your spouse, child, friend; why don't you always see eye to eye?"

One of my big secret reasons I keep promoting what I call my "Therapy For Therapy Horses" exercises, and all that Peggy Cummings and Linda Tellington-Jones teach, is by doing those exercises you will learn to hear your horse, as you wait, watch and listen for your horse's release and response. NOTE – To see photos of these exercises, please go to the "Exercises to Help Your Horse ... And You" section where you'll find these and other exercises described with photos.

Horse communication is not about "getting your horse to do something." If you approach your horse with a demanding attitude, desire or intent, you'll simply get static. Communication is about hearing what is important to the horse, so you can love more deeply, help more richly and understand more fully. That's it. It's that simple, and anyone can do it. In fact, even an inflexible non-believer is communicating with their horse. But sadly, those individuals are broadcasting, they don't care, so why would their horse talk to them?

Horse communication is all about listening, trusting and believing. Start by simply believing the thoughts you feel. Doubt builds walls. Believing builds conduits. Will you always get it right? Nope. But then again, do you always understand people? I reckon not. However, by accepting what you hear and feel, your intuition will strengthen. The thoughts, feelings and pictures will become more and more clear. It takes practice, as does learning any new language or skill. If someone wants to learn to play the guitar, they won't get very far without practice.

Back to the therapy exercises. Begin by doing them, and listening. You'll be amazed at what you hear. Your horse will guide your hands, really. Listen for the instruction. I like to suggest this, because it combines physical exercises and mental exercises. Add to this, the thought of listening to your horse in everything you do together, riding, groundwork, feeding, whatever. As you interact allow your mind to wonder into your horse's thoughts. Hear what is important to your horse. The louder you listen, the louder they'll talk. Set aside your wants, and listen.

Another nifty exercise to increase your hearing is simply sitting with your horse, and asking what is important to her. As you hear/feel what she is saying, see the picture. Let the scene build; softly focus on the center of the picture. Trust it, and see where it takes you. This one is fun, it only requires you allow the time for the scene to build. Be patient.

Trust in yourself, believe, and continue to learn. How far will it go? It's different for everyone. It's also wonderful for everyone. Kessy and I encourage you to explore horse communication. It'll change your life.

Gitty Up ~ *Dutch Henry*

Let Your Horse Help You See the Moment

Howdy Friends,

During these past few weeks of what I like to call a throwback winter, I often chuckle at folks posting countdowns to the first day of Spring, and friends calling to assure me they've had enough of this cold Winter. Soon enough it'll be Spring, and I do love the budding leaves, wildflowers and Spring songs of courting birds. And glorious Spring rides through the woods. But we've got some mighty fine Winter left to enjoy, too. I asked Kessy about longing for Spring, she took a deep breath, and let go a sigh, then rubbed her head against me.

On the heels of Spring comes Summer, the heat, the horseflies, ticks and fleas. And the yard and garden work and play. Folks will then be posting about the heat, the horseflies, fleas and ticks, and counting down to Fall. I asked Kessy how she feels about Summer. She took a deep breath, let go a sigh, took a bite of hay and gazed out over the snow-covered forest floor. Then she rubbed her head on my arm.

Fall will come, leaves will change, the forest will look spectacular. Days will shorten, the moon will hang larger in the sky, and gardens will show signs of wear. I asked Kessy what she thought of Autumn. She took a deep breath, looked out at the snow, then rubbed her head on my shoulder.

Of course as Fall wears on, the days not only get shorter, but colder too. Mostly the horseflies, mosquitoes and ticks go their way, away from us, hiding from the cold about to embrace us. Then Winter pays us a visit, bringing along her friends cold, snow, ice and Mr. Blustery Wind. Folks start longing for Spring, talking and writing how they're ready to be finished with Old Man Winter. It seems whatever season we're in, folks long for the next one. Living months ahead of themselves, instead of enjoying the moment they're in. I asked Kessy how she felt about Winter, she took a bite of hay and munched away. Then she rubbed her head on my shoulder.

I like to write about our weather, too. In fact I have lots of fun with it, and love sharing the moment and descriptions with our Coffee Clutch and Facebook friends. I enjoy each season we're in, from the high heat of Summer to the low cold of Winter. I cherish each moment, live in it. Find the beauty and fun in it. Kessy and other horses taught me that. When you get anxious, worried or frustrated, let your horse help you see the moment. Let her rub off on you.

Gitty Up ~ *Dutch Henry*

Let Your Horse Understand You

——⟨✿⟩——

Howdy Friends,

Does your horse understand you? Have you spent the time, not teaching her or "training" her, but simply allowing her to understand you? Recently I spent the evening watching a versatility show and noticed riders operating in a different realm than their horses. I noticed too how some riders seemed to possess two different personalities. One personality outside the ring while awaiting their turn, and a totally different one inside.

We hear so much about bonding, partnering and "joining up" with our horses, and too often what's forgotten is simple understanding. Before you and your horse can truly bond, she needs to understand you. Sure she understands your signals, cues, and you think you understand her, but have you really allowed her to understand you?

There is a huge difference between a horse cooperating with their person and one who truly understands their person. Remember, a horse is very quick to read us and understand our attitude, posture and motives, and these barriers could prohibit them from deeply understanding their person.

What do I mean by understanding us? Think about your friends and family, do they always communicate in the same manner with you? Do you with them? But when they do something that seems out of character, you realize it's out of character and "understand" them. You understand they may be upset, anxious, even hurt or angry. You understand they are not displaying their true inner being in that moment, and you take it in stride.

Sure, when you act "out of character" with your horse, they will respond, obey, even cooperate, but it will also confuse them. And each time we do this, it chips away a tiny bit of their trust in us. Think about friends you might have, around whom you sometime feel as if you must "walk on eggshells." That is the feeling your horse will develop around you, if you haven't taken the time to allow them to truly understand you.

It's easy to help your horse truly understand you and requires no special training, clinics or instructors. First, we must truly want our horse to understand us, in our hearts and thoughts. Second, we must spend time, a good deal of it, just being with them. Not feeding, grooming, riding or training—just being in their company. Walk with her, sit with her and, very important, talk with her. Slow down, allow her to come to you, mentally. The neat thing is, as she begins to understand you more deeply, you will understand her as well. That, then, is a true partnership, and when folks watch you and your horse they'll see two beings so in sync they act as one rather than two beings each operating in their own realm. This tiny shift in perspective works wonders—try it and see for yourself!

Gitty Up ~ *Dutch Henry*

Let's Think With Our Horses

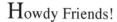

Howdy Friends!

Heavy hung over the day. Clouds blocked the sun and gripped her thoughts and heart. Work was not going well, and other decisions must be made. She'd be late today, wouldn't matter anyway, so she dragged her feet as she made her way to the barn. Before she opened the door, a soft nicker greeted her. Before she opened the door, her heart lifted. A smile forced its way to her face. She flung open the door with more purpose than she thought she could muster, and went inside to her thinking place ... with her horses.

We've all done this, carried our woes, sorrows and issues like backpacks strapped to our hearts. Friends, spouses and our children can all help, and surely they do. Dogs and cats too, I can't imagine a life without them. But horses—the magic their spirit has to lift and understand ours is as unique as it is powerful. All we need do is think with them. They will hear us.

How many times have we all pondered a question, or some difficult issue while riding, grooming or simply sitting with our horses, to have an answer mysteriously weave its way through our internal fog? We've all experienced it. Is it a coincidence? Some would suggest yes. I subscribe to a different belief.

We need ask nothing of them. We need only to allow the connection. We've all heard and read the stories of wonderful healing places where horses do the healing. I've written about dozens of them myself.

There is a sweet power in the way a horse can touch our consciousness, even our sub-consciousness.

Do they send us ideas, or do they simply empower us to solve our problems, to celebrate our joys?

I say, you bet!

I promise you—it's great to take your contemplations to the barn. "Let's think with our horses."

Gitty Up ~ *Dutch Henry*

When Your Horse Asks a Question, How Do You Reply?

Howdy Folks,

How do you respond when your horse asks a question? You might be surprised to learn a lot of folks don't even know their horses can and often do ask questions. So how can they respond to a question they don't know is being asked?

Imagine you and your spouse or a good friend are planning to go to the movies. You've talked about it, now it's time. You innocently ask, "Are we ready to go?" To your surprise the response is a sharp-toned "Stand still until I tell you to move!" Of course we all know this is a harsh example and no one talks to spouses, friends or horses this way. Surely not.

But what if your question was "Is this cake still good to eat?" and the answer came back, "Eat what I put in front of you!"

Horses ask questions all the time and many times they go unanswered, or the answers come unrelated to the question. Suppose you ask, "What time does 'Dancing With the Stars' come on?" and you're told, "Wash the car before the rain starts." Hard to make sense of that one, I reckon.

How do you know if your horse is asking a question? If we're listening, they tell us in many little ways. Horses by their very nature are full of questions, but too many times they're taught their questions are unimportant or worse, the act of asking a question is considered a discipline or training problem.

Just like us, horses want to be happy. They have a desire to please. And they think a lot. They are better than most folks at noticing things—things they want to investigate, things they love, things they worry about. We have a responsibility as owners, caregivers and partners to be there for our horses. When they ask a question that's important to them, it should be important to us as well.

Just as for us sometimes, the answer to your horse's question may not be the answer she wants, but we should at least take the time to answer it. Politely. And sometimes it'll be exactly the answer she's looking for.

How can we hear a question? When she hesitates at a cue or a request, she's asking. Listen. Look in her eyes. Trust your thoughts, your intuition. It's extremely important to not be negative or demanding at this moment. Your first thought, in a positive manner, will be the answer to her question. Tell her. Yes you can speak just as you would to anyone who asked a question. Tell her what she needs to know, and perhaps show her. Think of opening the way and allowing her to follow through.

The neat thing about listening for questions is that the more you do it, the better you'll become. You'll learn from each other and learn, brick by brick, to trust each other. Questions are good things, we learn by asking. So do our horses. Reward the asking in a positive way, and anything you would like to do together is possible.

Gitty Up ~ *Dutch Henry*

SECTION II

Exersizes To Help Your Horse And You

In this section, you'll find stories about exercises that promote proper and healthy posture, body carriage and awareness for your horse, and they do even more than that. As you play with and master the simple techniques we'll chat about here, you will learn to hear your horse in ways you may have never imagined.

Be sure to allow your horse to guide you. Everything I do, and explain here, including what I call my "Therapy For Therapy Horses" exercises, I learned from my years of working with my mentor Diane Sept, a Senior Certified Connected Riding Instructor®. Among them are the techniques of Peggy Cummings' Connected Riding and Groundwork® and Linda Tellington-Jones' Tellington TTouch®.

I will reference Peggy and Linda and their techniques, and I highly recommend you purchase their books and DVDs. You will find their web addresses in the reference section near the end of the book.

Why "Therapy For Therapy Horses"?

Howdy Friends,

Friends new to our Facebook page and Coffee Clutch blog may not be sure what "Therapy For Therapy Horses" is, or why I created this simple program, or the free clinics, so I figured it was time to dust off the old story and explain. It started years ago when I was working with my mentor, Diane Sept, a Senior Certified Connected Riding Instructor®, learning many things about horses, and myself, and helping to rehabilitate Tennessee Walking Horses from the show world.

During those years, I learned much from Diane and the horses, most notably the biomechanics of the horse and techniques of Peggy Cummings Connected Riding and Groundwork® and Linda Tellington-Jones' Tellington TTouch®. Peggy and Linda (as well as Sally Swift and her Centered Riding techniques) are true pioneers—they have changed the horse world, and I highly recommend you purchase their books and DVDs.

When I began writing about "People and Horses Helping Horses and People" for equine magazines shortly after moving to Virginia, I wrote more than a few stories about therapeutic riding centers, and the magic that happens there. Over the years, my health has had its ups and downs, and the first stories I did by way of phone interviews, as travel was a tad difficult. Then I decided I wanted to witness the magic firsthand and visited the next therapeutic riding center to do my interview. I had for decades already known, felt and understood the healing power of the spirit of the horse, and I wanted to thank in person the horses who shared it so freely.

One day while visiting a very nice and popular therapeutic riding center for an interview for their story, I could see that the horses, while well cared for, had a stiffness about them. Upon closer examination, I noticed several of the horses were heavy on their forehand, inverted and weak in the hind end. As part of the interview, I watched a few therapy sessions and noticed some of the horses moving with short, choppy strides and having difficulty turning smoothly. This came as a surprise to me.

I did witness magic, and lots of it, on my first in-person interview! And as I wrote their story, I was reminded of the excitement on the children's and volunteers' faces. For one little boy it was the first time he'd ever caught a ball. How we cheered! I still get teary-eyed thinking of it. I decided what I thought I saw in the horses was actually me not really "getting it" ... Yet the horses tugged at me.

Over the next few months, I had the opportunity to visit several more equine assisted therapy centers for in-person interviews. I visited centers with both children and adult participants. With horses purchased specifically because their breed enjoys reputations as great therapy horses and centers operating with all donated horses, as well as a mixture of both. Every place I visited was a happy place. Clean, well-managed barns. Well kept, well fed horses. Wonderfully polite and knowledgeable staff and volunteers. And thrilling, lively and eager participants. I had several great stories to write celebrating the wonderful things that happened in those barns on the backs of and from the hearts of those loving horses.

I did, however, begin to notice in too many of the horses, the same stiffness and discomfort I thought

I saw earlier. Unsettled, I did some checking and discovered that yes indeed, often horses who do equine assisted therapy develop a few kinks in their bodies. And in fairness, any horse doing the same job repeatedly does too. Even lesson horses and show horses can become a little stiff or locked up here or there—they are just more likely to let us know they are unhappy about something. But most therapy horses have that frame of mind that they will endure and not show their discomfort too boldly. That personality trait of caring more for others than themselves is exactly the trait that makes them good therapy horses.

Therapy horses take their jobs seriously. From the interviews I've conducted, most folks who know say only about one horse in 25 or 30 has what it takes to become a therapy horse. They have a happy but demanding job, and need to possess a way of thinking that puts others first. Therapy horses carry precious cargo, and much is expected of them. As they walk along giving healing therapy, they must not only be aware of that precious cargo, who may not be able to sit correctly, use their legs or concentrate, but they must also be careful not to bump the sidewalkers, one on each side. The leader and therapist too must be accounted for with each step. This can sometimes cause the horse to move in ways that tweak its spine, neck, withers or hips. Often equine assisted therapy programs include exercises for the participant to do while sitting on the horse at a standstill, such as upper body calisthenics, shooting basketball or playing catch. This can be very stressful on a horse's back. Many times therapy horses are donated horses because they've had an injury that forced them out of their careers, so they may also need to compensate for them too. Since many times the centers are working with donated tack as well, it is not unusual for therapy horses to perform their miracles in tack that does not quite fit.

Just as I was compelled to write the stories of "People and Horses Helping Horses and People," I felt compelled to see how I might be able to help the therapy horses in some way. I visited a few more centers and kept a keen eye on the horses' movements and attitudes. What I had earlier suspected seemed to be true. Too often, the horses were heavy on their forehand, inverted and weak in the hind end. I even saw horses who protested by nipping the leaders or shaking their heads. From my training and work with Diane Sept, I could easily recognize what was wrong and had thoughts about how to help. The exercises she had taught me years earlier based on the teachings of Peggy Cummings and Linda Tellington-Jones were all that was needed.

But understanding how full every day is at most equine assisted therapy centers, how would adding extra duties to their day be a benefit? I called Diane, as I often do for advice, and as luck would have it, she was just a week away from presenting a short refresher clinic on many of the basic Connected Groundwork exercises. Perfect! Over the weekend she coached me and helped select the exercises that were most beneficial to the therapy horses and easy to learn for volunteers. Most can be worked into the center's regular routine, adding very little time to already overloaded schedules. This was great, because no exercise is worth anything if it's not practiced.

Armed with Diane's suggestions and advice, I put together what I call my "Therapy For Therapy Horses" clinics, a series of easy-to-do and easy-to-learn exercises for both people and horses, and began to offer them free of charge (I do ask for travel expenses) to Equine Assisted Therapy Centers. These exercises help the horses release and relax, carry themselves off their forehand, lift their back, soften their inversion muscles and engage the hind end into a soft, long stride. Equine assisted therapy is very taxing mentally on horses, and I'm not sure enough people understand that. Another benefit of these simple exercises is the mental release the horse enjoys along with a renewed ability to focus.

While assembled for the therapy horses, this series of exercises is perfect for all horses and all horse caregivers, and if I could have one wish, it would be that every horse caregiver master them. Well maybe two wishes, the second being that every therapeutic riding center would understand that therapy horses need a little therapy too.

Gitty Up ~ *Dutch Henry*

An Easy Exercise to Relax and Release Your Horse Anytime

Howdy Folks,

This is a simple little exercise you can do anytime at all. It is a wonderful, relaxing exercise that asks absolutely nothing of your horse. It is totally giving to the horse. All the exercises I promote give to the horse, which is so very important. Some exercises do require the horse participate with movement and thinking, and that is often very important, healing and beneficial. This little ditty requires nothing of the horse, except that they enjoy it.

The first thing I'd like to show is the "Mane Wiggle." Stand beside your horse in a neutral, relaxed posture; grasp her mane in one hand and lift just enough to create a connection, and wiggle your hand, and her mane and neck, gently. As you wiggle, you'll see her neck loosen and begin to wiggle, and she may slowly drop her head. She will begin to loosen and wiggle through her neck to her face, and also back through her withers, shoulders and beyond. This is very relaxing, and you can do it often.

The second exercise I call the "Forelock Wiggle." Again, stand by your horse in neutral and relaxed, grasp her forelock, lift gently and wiggle. Watch for the release of her neck, face and jaw. Her bottom lip will release and wiggle.

Next let's do the "Tail Hair" wiggle. Relaxed and in neutral, stand behind your horse, grasp some tail hair near the base of the tail, and wiggle. This will release the tail—the end of her spine—all the way to her sacral joint, and even more.

I hope you will incorporate these easy and fun exercises into your regular routine. These little wiggles really give a wonderful gift to your horse, and not only release and relax, but you can use the "Mane Wiggle" when you need to calm your horse. They love it.

Gitty Up ~ *Dutch Henry*

SEEING WITH HER FEET

Kessy's left front and right rear legs have "stepped back."
She has also immediately adjusted into "rock back." Notice
how she is off her forehand and has her weight shifted to her
hind end in correct posture.

"Seeing With Her Feet"
A One-Step Exercise to Help Your Horse Find Her Feet

————◇————

Howdy Friends,

A very important and easy thing you can do to help your horse maintain proper posture, soft body carriage and self-awareness as well as self-confidence is a little exercise known as the "One-Step." This is so easy to learn and do and will make a huge difference in not only the areas I've already mentioned, but your horse will start your ride relaxed and confident, too.

You see, because of the things we ask our horses to do, they often lose connection with their feet. They have that momentum thing down all right. They're going from here to there, but that's just it, it's all about momentum. They see the rail, the jump, the turn in the trail, the cavaletti, the barrels—they see it all, and they're going where you send them. But their energy, their momentum, is flying ahead, and they are often not aware of their feet. Sometimes they stumble, trip, overstride or get pushy as you lead. It's not their fault; *it's not a training or discipline issue.* It's a physical issue. They honestly don't know where their feet are. They are unable to "see with their feet," because they don't know where they are. This exercise will help fix that.

Stand in front of your horse holding the lead softly, and simply ask for "One Step Forward," then stop, and rock her back off one step off the forehand. Let her stand and process that feeling of lightly taking only one easy step. One step is a complete step, and it includes one front and the alternate (diagonal) hind.

When you begin this exercise, she will most likely take more than one step, because she'll have the momentum started, just as she's been taught. That's okay, go with it—wherever she stops, tell her "good girl," and let her feel the softness. Then ask for "one step back," the same two feet you had asked her to step forward. Allow her to feel the softness, process the moment, and then ask for "one step forward" again—allow her to feel it, process it, congratulate her, then one step back again. Repeat forward and back 3 or 4 times, then switch to her other side and do it all over again. You should see her softening overall, and lowering her head. Remember, one step is a complete step, one front and alternate hind each time. Don't forget to allow time, every time, for her to process and feel the moment. And don't forget to rock her back off her forehand after each one-step.

This is one of the exercises I do every time before I step into the saddle or do any ground work. Once you and your horse master this, it'll be a fun and healthy game. You'll feel the difference in everything you do together.

Another great exercise to add is the "One Step Over a Row of Cavaletti." Lead your horse slowly over the cavaletti, but pause and rock back just before each one (Note: if the poles are spaced about 3 feet apart, your horse should step over one pole with each step). Allow a second or three at each pause for your horse to process. It won't take long until you will notice a difference in how your horse places her feet. When you've mastered this, back through the cavaletti, one step at a time.

The more you do the "One Step," the smoother, softer and more confident each step will become—in this exercise, and everywhere else as well. After all, you've helped her find her feet again. It's all about "seeing with her feet."

Kessy and I hope you'll make this fun exercise part of your routine. It also goes a long way to helping a horse look for soft cues. And helping us become softer in giving cues.

Gitty Up ~ *Dutch Henry*

Easy, Fun Stretches For Your Horse
For Restart or Any Time

─────◆〈✦〉◆─────

Howdy Friends,

Kessy and I have not been able to hit the trail since the last week of April because of my adventure in cardiac-land. We won't be enjoying saddle time or trails until September, but I've been given the okay to do a lot of things now, and I'm beginning to get Kessy ready for the big day. Bringing a healthy horse back from a 4-month "vacation" is certainly not as difficult as one that had been given rest due to injury, but I believe one should take care in the restart just the same. Even though she enjoys her big treed playground and run-in, I've not been able to do anything with Kessy for 3 months, except Coffee Clutch and brush her. She's had no bodywork, exercises or any of the things we hold so valuable. I even had a friend trim her feet! Still can't go back to that for 8 weeks.

Over the past few days, I've begun to do little things with Kessy to get her body in shape again, and one very important thing is to loosen her up with gentle, easy stretching exercises. These carrot exercises are for the horse to release in her own comfort zone, with no pressure, no stress. I recommend these for every horse all the time, but they are highly important to restarting a horse. Once you start doing them, you will be amazed at how much your horse changes.

Start by offering a carrot on the left and right sides; hold your hand somewhere near her side so she reaches for the carrot.

Two things are important: she must not step to come for it, and don't ask for too big of a bend at first.

Some horses will bend all the way to their ribs the first time, others will only be able to come half way or less. **Whatever suits your horse is best—keep it comfortable.**

CARROT STRETCH

This is all you need to do every day for a few days until she can do this with ease on both sides. Then you can add the **Carrot Bow**.

To do the Carrot Bow, reach between her front legs and encourage her to bow to reach for it. **At first she may not be able to bow very far, so don't push it— reach up to her, keep her comfortable.**

CARROT BOW

Gradual increases in reach over a few days will get her all the way. Then you can add the **Big Stretch Carrot.**

To do the Big Stretch Carrot, your horse must be able to do the side and bow carrots with great ease. Start with them each day, then when she is ready, stand toward her rear, reach between her hind legs up to her toward her belly and encourage her to reach back and under to her groin for the carrot. At first she may be confused, side step, try to turn to get it. Be consistent with your encouragement, and ask her to stand still and reach with her neck to accomplish the stretch. If you have given enough days and time to the side and bow stretches she will be able to do the big stretch the first or second time you try, **but don't rush it.**

Be sure to do these stretches at liberty, with no halter or lead line. She must be free to release, relax and stretch. *Don't hurry the process—give each exercise the days it takes to master.* Just because your horse snatches the carrot, if she is fast and struggling to grab it, she has not mastered the release, so slow down and watch for the graceful move. After you and your horse have mastered them, make them a part of your pre-ride warm up. Kessy and I hope you enjoy these stretches, and joining us on our trail-riding restart. From time to time, we'll share more restart exercises.

Gitty Up ~ *Dutch Henry*

BIG STRETCH CARROT

Neat Little Lesson Horse
(Or Any Horse) Exercise

Howdy Friends,

One day while working with the therapy horses, I was asked about one of the lesson horses not in the therapeutic riding program. He's a little Appaloosa named Freckles. Freckles had begun to buck a hop or two whenever a student asked for a canter.

Lesson horses, just as therapy horses, work very hard and are of a special, gentle, forgiving nature. Day after day, lesson horses are asked to go around the ring at a walk, trot or gait, and canter on cue. Very often the student doing the asking is just learning how to ask or cue. They may not have mastered a gentle touch, or may be too timid. All lesson horses at some point teach students how to ask for the "whoa, back-up and walk on," while perhaps at the same time the student is finding their seat, or balanced posture. Along with love and admiration (who hasn't fallen in love with their lesson horse?) are confusing signals, heavy hands on bits and repetitious routines. They are, for the most part, simply part of a lesson horse's life.

Sometimes they just get a little stuck and need a break—a fun trail ride or some other kind of interesting activity to engage them, just as we do. And most instructors are keenly aware of this and make sure to get some variety in the their lesson horses' routines. The center I was at is very good at this, but Freckles was trying to tell us more. All the normal things had been gone over—tack fit, time off, etc., and still whenever he was asked to canter, he would give those little hops.

First I did a few of my regular "Therapy For Therapy Horses" exercises because by doing them I can almost always begin to tune in to the horse's needs. It felt as if Freckles was tight in the left side and hip. I worked a bit to loosen him, especially his hind end and legs.

Now here is the neat little exercise I ended with and Freckles responded nicely, as all horses will.

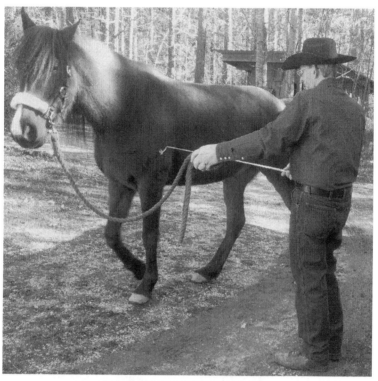

INSIDE SHOULDER UP

On a long lead, ask your horse to walk in an easy circle. At first, walk closely alongside her, about an arm's length away. As you circle together, use your wand to ask her to keep the "inside shoulder up." If you watch closely, you'll often see a horse lean in and drop the inside shoulder. As you walk, "tap, tap" the inside shoulder until she learns to hold it up. In a few moments (sometimes it takes longer, so don't get discouraged) you can begin to just point with your wand and she'll hold her shoulder up.

To begin the "inside shoulder up" exercises, your horse must be willing to walk on softly and quietly on your short lead in a circle. Stay as near her as you need to encourage her and support her, and begin to introduce the wand in a way that she recognizes and is comfortable with. Here I am lightly taping Kessy's shoulder and she is holding correct posture even as she begins a turn. It may take some time to master this, so do not hurry to move to a long line until this short line exercise is totally mastered by both of you.

When you've mastered that, begin to back away, making the circle larger and larger while being careful to keep the inside shoulder up. When you've backed away about 12 feet and completed a few successful circles at a slow walk, begin to slowly reel her in, making the circle smaller and smaller. *Remember to use your wand to keep the inside shoulder up*. Then send her out again. After a few times of expanding and contracting the circle, switch to the other side and repeat the entire process. *I only ever do this at a walk*. But you must keep this posture in mind when and if you trot or gait on the longe line. The inside shoulder must always be up—and it is your responsibility to help your horse with that.

It's a neat little exercise that helps any horse be more aware of their body carriage and helps make transitions smooth as silk. I hope you'll try it! Your horse is counting on you.

Gitty Up ~ *Dutch Henry*

Pre-Ride Exercises

━━━◆◇◆━━━

Howdy Friends,

How often do we see horses fetched from the pasture, stall or trailer and hurriedly saddled, then folks just mount up and ride away? Often these horses are "up" and moving out in a hurry, so the rider shifts gears to discipline. In my humble opinion, that's not fair to the horse. And the situation can be made so much better with a few easy-to-do pre-ride exercises. Part of the tacking-up time should be giving to your horse, too.

The first thing I do when I go to Kessy is ask her to put her head down for the halter. Horses should always lower their head for you. It is polite to you, and actually feels good to them. It is easy to teach, and if you are having any difficulties with this, please email me. At this time I do a few "Poll Wiggles." Lightly place your fingers around the poll and wiggle, just enough that would jiggle a bowl of Jell-O. Your horse may ask for more vigor, so go for it, gently.

Then while she stands ground tied, I do a row of TTouch® circles starting at the side of her neck in the thickest muscle, going all along her back about 2 inches down from the spine, through her croup and down her thigh muscles on both sides. It will take about a minute per side. Kessy can come and go as she pleases and is usually outside for these, then we walk to the barn to brush and tack. On the walk, I do a serpentine path, good for their legs and back. I feel you should rarely walk your horse in a straight line; serpentine is always better. If you've trailered to ride, before you tie to tack, take a short walk doing the serpentine walk. Horses really appreciate a little walk after a trailer ride.

When we get to the barn, I lift each leg about halfway up, hold it a second waiting for the release, do little circles, then set it down. Don't just let go, but set it down. Softly. Then I ask for the back lift, hold a few seconds and release, again slowly. Then I'll saddle her, for now keeping the girth loose, not yet snug.

Before I put on her riding halter (just a rope halter with reins for us—Kessy has never had a bit in her mouth or shoes on her feet), I do the "Cheek Wiggle." Place your left hand on the noseband, slip your fingers of your right hand under her cheek, lightly grip and wiggle gently for a few seconds. Repeat on the other side. Then the halter goes on and I check the girth, do the "one step" and "rock back."

NOTE – To see photos of these exercises, please go to the **"Restarting, Conditioning and Great Exercises For Your Horse Pt 1, 2, 3, 4"** section in this chapter where you'll find these and other exercises described with photos.

On the way to the mounting block, I ask for a few circles, left and right, at a walk and keeping the inside shoulder up (very important). I finish the girth, move to the mounting block, and step up. One last important exercise: The first step should always be a "lateral step," not straight on, after she reaches back for a carrot at her stirrup on each side.

A big benefit to doing these, aside from the relaxing and bonding, is if you make it positively routine, when you are away somewhere and stick to the routine, your horse will have a familiar feeling. It will build confidence before you ever start on the trail.

Kessy and I hope you'll make this part of your pre-ride. Feel free to ask questions. There are others, perhaps I'll blog later about them, but these are the ones I do without fail.

Gitty Up ~ *Dutch Henry*

Restarting, Conditioning and Great Exercises For Your Horse Pt 1

(Includes the "Therapy for Therapy Horses" Exercises)

Howdy Friends,

Let's see, in 6 days Kessy and I can ride again. Our last trail adventure was Sunday, April 27 … Gosh that seems like a long time ago! We had just that day started a new way of going, no reins, but then we were interrupted by my cardiac adventure. Now friends, when a horse has been idle for that long (5 months), even though she has 24/7 turnout in a modified Paddock Paradise track system, I don't believe you should just saddle up and go. It's important for the health and mental wellbeing of your horse to get them back in shape for rides; a horse loses his cardio fitness in about 30 days, muscles about the same, and tendon and bone in about 90 days.

I started Kessy's restart 2 weeks ago with carrot stretches, and shared them on our Coffee Clutch blog. This weekend I started relax, release and body, foot and posture awareness exercises. Ravishin' Robbie took some photos and I'll be writing a series of posts to share them with you. Our first rides next week will be 15-20 minutes over the same course I walked for my cardio rehab. The following week, we'll add time and a little terrain change. The week after that we'll add more distance and more terrain change. It takes about 30 days to get a previously unconditioned horse minimally fit…when I trained for CTR and endurance, I learned it takes 60 days for cardio, 90- 120 for muscle and a year or longer for bone and tendon to condition. Kessy and I hope you'll enjoy our Coffee Clutch series, "Restarting, Conditioning and Great Exercises For Your Horse."

We'll start by reviewing, over three days, relax, release and body, foot and posture awareness exercises I learned while working with my mentor Diane Sept for nearly a decade. From Diane, a Senior Certified Connected Riding Instructor, I learned the techniques of Peggy Cummings, Connected Riding and Ground Work® and Linda Tellington Jones, Tellington TTouch Training ™ . I highly recommend their training and books. In their books you'll find these and many more excellent exercises.

The exercises we'll discuss and explore are excellent for restarting a horse, but I recommend them as part of everyday routines for all horses. We will cover more than you need to do every day, but some I do faithfully before I tack up, every time, no exception. In time you'll learn to hear your horse when she tells you which ones she really needs. All of these

exercises, about a dozen, are the basis for what I call my "Therapy For Therapy Horses" clinics.

Today's exercises I call the "Top-Line" exercises I always do before I tacking up. It's important to note, always do these ground tied or in a stall so the horse is free to move. Have no hay or grass in your exercise area—you want them focused on you and their release. Do not discipline during exercises as that will short-circuit any release. Be sure to watch for and allow sighs, licks and chews. Your horse may ask for a little walk to absorb and process these new sensations, so walk them, if they ask, for a minute, then begin again.

We'll start with the **Poll Wiggle.**

Gently support her head by holding the halter. Place your fingertips around the poll, and watch for the release as you wiggle gently. I always start with this, and it is great to do anytime. It will also help calm a horse anytime.

Next is a series of Tellington TTouch exercises along the back, about 2 inches below the spine and rump, both sides. You can also do them on each side of the neck.

POLL WIGGLE

The circles are about the size of a quarter, moving clockwise with your fingertips of one hand, resting the heel for support, your hand cupped, letting your fingertips do the work. As you picture the clock face, start at 6 move to 9, 12, 3, back to 6 and on to 9 and stop there, making a circle and a quarter. Slide your hand about 2 inches and do the next circle, and so on. Pressure is gentle, just enough to move (not rub) the skin. Make a series of circles all along the back, out over the rump and down the meaty part of the thigh on both sides, with your line about 3 inches from the spine. Always maintain a connection with both hands—i.e., if you are making the connected circles with your right hand, keep your left hand resting lightly on the chest or withers. When you're finished, lay both hands over the horse flat and gently drag them over your tracks. (I often do this one first out in the field before I even halter Kessy.)

Next, the **Vertebrae Wiggle**

Starting at the poll, using your fingertips, grasp each vertebra and wiggle each one a time or two. Imagine holding the vertebrae in your fingers and moving one hand away from you while pulling the other to you so it wiggles. Proceed all the way down the neck, across the back, over the croup (I know you can't feel the spine here, so just pretend you can) and down the tail—where the wiggle is up and down, not back and forth. If your horse clamps her tail, gently slide your fingers under her tail and tickle until she lifts it. In time this will not be an issue. In addition, many horses hold much tension in their tails so you must be very gentle. This exercise will ease that tension and relax the entire horse in a way that is lasting.

VERTEBRAE WIGGLE

Next, the **Tail Pull**

Grasp the tail about midpoint and by bending your knees pull slowly, steadily and firmly, being very careful to stay on the angle of her croup, as I am here with Kessy, and hold the pressure a few seconds as she tightens her rump, engages her abdomen and raises her back. Then release very slowly.

TAIL PULL

Next, the **Belly/Back Lift**

Standing beside your horse, reach under exactly in the middle, front to rear and side to side, and with your fingernails, in a slow steady motion, apply pressure until she engages her abdomen (and you can see in this photo how much Kessy has engaged her abdomen) and lifts her back. Hold this for a few seconds and release SLOWLY ...

Note, this exercise MUST be done AFTER all the Top-Line release exercises are completed, not before or as a lone exercise.

BELLY/BACK LIFT

In time, when your horse is released, and used to carrying herself in proper released and relaxed posture, you can do the Belly/Back Lift anytime, and should do it often.

Kessy and I hope you'll make these easy exercises part of your routine. Tomorrow we'll move into a few great body release and relax exercises.

Gitty Up ~ *Dutch Henry*

Restarting, Conditioning and Great Exercises For Your Horse Pt 2

(Includes the "Therapy for Therapy Horses" Exercises)

Howdy Friends,

Yesterday we talked about the importance of restarting a horse after time off and learned about the Top-Line release and relax exercises, which I like to suggest become a part of every horse caregiver's routine. Today we'll have a look at exercises for the body and legs. It's important to note—always do these ground tied or in a stall so the horse is free to move. Have no hay or grass in your exercise area; you want them focused on you and their release. Do not discipline during exercises, as that will short-circuit any release. Be sure to watch for and allow sighs, licks and chews. Your horse may ask for a little walk to absorb these new feelings, so walk them if they ask for a minute, then begin again.

After I do the Top-Line I move to the front legs with the **Armpit Release**. This exercise will begin to release the tension in the chest muscles, and helps with girthy horses, and begins the reconnection to their feet. Remember, do both sides.

Stand straddling her leg, in neutral position with your knees slightly bent. Place your palms inside her leg and gently slide your hands up into her armpit, keeping your palms against her leg. Keep gently pushing up, allowing her to release the tension in her muscles and continue to move into the space opened by her release until you can go no further, then release slowly. Note—some horses are so tight they may try to bite, so you made need to first get her used to your

ARMPIT RELEASE

hands touching the inside of her leg, then in time move your hands into her armpit.

Next, the **Shoulder Delineation**

This exercise will release the tension along the base of the neck, withers and forehand, and begin to correct the inversion muscles and help maintain proper soft posture.

Immediately following Armpit Release, leaving one hand in the armpit, with your other hand search for the crease in the center of the chest muscles on this leg, not the center of the chest, starting at the base. When you find the crease (in the beginning this could be hard to find, you may need to make it) gently work your fingers in, and walk up the crease toward the neck. (You can see Kessy's crease go deep, but be gentle) Then bring your other hand up to help, and "walk" them both upward, using fingers to find the crease between neck and shoulder. Continue up over and around the shoulder back down to her armpit.

In many spots you may not find a crease; many horses are so tight from poor posture, stress and even tack and riding that it may take time to develop the looseness, but it will come.

SHOULDER DELINEATION

Remember to do both sides. Often, the horse will turn her head toward you in an attempt to release the crease, and that's a good thing.

Next, the **Pretty Neck** (inversion muscle release) exercise

This exercise will release the tension in the neck muscles and bones and poll. It also begins to correct the inverted neck and tight chest muscles, allows for free-flowing movement and aids in getting horses off their forehand. (As you might guess, I'm very anti tie-down, and these exercises mentioned so far today will help eliminate the need for them.) Remember to do both sides.

Look at her chest just below the neck for the muscle we call the inversion muscle. It will appear as a vertical muscle just about where the neck meets the chest, some are easy to see, others not. Gently grasp the muscle as I do here, and squeeze from the BOTTOM up, like milking backwards. Watch for her to arch her neck like Kessy is here. Some horses will back up, because they think you're asking for that, or sometimes they are so tight and sore they can't arch their neck. I like to rest my hand on their withers to give them support. Just walk with her and keep trying and in a few seconds, if your hand is at the correct place, and you're squeezing from the bottom, you'll see an attempt. Release quickly. But when she begins to master it, hold a few more seconds so she can get the big release. In time she will soften, and soften and give you beautiful stretch and release. Remember, do both sides.

PRETTY NECK

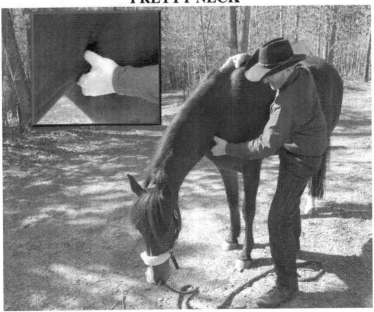

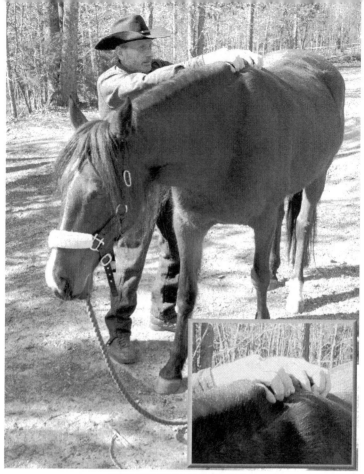

WHITHERS ROCK

Next, the **Withers Rock**

This exercise releases the shoulders, neck and spine and aids in free flowing movement and balance.

Stand beside your horse with both hands resting on the withers and gently wiggle, not moving the horse, just wiggling her withers. Then start over and ever so gently rock her back and forth about 5 times. We are not looking for big movement, just enough to see her shift her body but not her feet. Think of a swaying motion, but less.

Next, the **Shoulder Circles**

This exercise releases tension in the shoulders, chest, neck and withers, creates soft fluid strides and increases body awareness, balance and posture.

Hold her leg near the knee and fetlock and trace about 5 small, gentle circles left and right. Allow no movement in the knee as this could cause damage; we are looking for movement in the shoulder. Be sure to stay under her shoulder, don't pull it toward you. When finished, set her foot down, don't drop it. Remember to do both sides.

SHOULDER CIRCLES

Tomorrow we'll look at a few exercises for the hind legs and body posture and correct soft carriage.

Gitty Up ~ *Dutch Henry*

Restarting, Conditioning and Great Exercises For Your Horse Pt 3

(Includes the Therapy for Therapy Horses Exercises)

Howdy Friends,

In Pt 1 we talked about the importance of restarting a horse after time off and learned about the Top-Line release and relax exercises, which I like to suggest become a part of every horse caregiver's routine. In Pt 2 we looked at exercises for the body and front legs. Today we'll learn exercises for the hind legs and a few in-motion exercises to work on posture, balance and connection to her feet. It's important to note, always do these ground tied so the horse is free to move. Have no hay or grass in your exercise area, you want them focused on you and their release. Do not discipline during exercises, as that will short-circuit any release. Be sure to watch for and allow sighs, licks and chews. Your horse may ask for a little walk to absorb these new sensations, walk them for a minute if they ask, then begin again.

All the exercises we've covered so far, I do in the order we are discussing them, including the ones we'll learn today. The routine takes me 40 minutes. I recommend you do all of them every day starting at least 2 weeks before you restart a horse. Don't forget the carrot stretches. And continue the entire routine while conditioning or restarting your horse. We'll talk more about that in Pt 4. I'm not a fan of longeing or round penning. I include neither in my conditioning, restarting or routine maintenance. I don't have a riding ring or round pen. I believe the best conditioning, physical and mental, for any

GROIN RELEASE

discipline, is on the trail. We'll revisit that in Pt 4 too. These exercises done pre-ride do more to warm up and ready a horse than any longeing can, in my opinion. As time goes on and your horse becomes balanced, fit and relaxed, you can begin to streamline your exercises to doing only a few every time pre-ride and keep the others in your tool box for every now and then. I never ride without doing the top-line routine (and the rock back and one step, which you'll learn today).

When I finish in the front, I move to the rear with the **Groin Release**. This exercise releases and relaxes the thick muscles of the hind end. It is very important for a free flowing stride and correct relaxed posture.

Just as with the Armpit Release, stand straddling the hind leg, place your palm on the inside of her thigh and slide your hand up into her groin. Keep pressure on and move in deeper as she releases muscle until you can go no further, then hold and release slowly. Remember to do both sides. Some horses love this, others will have no part of it, so begin with care and just place one hand on the inside thigh to see what your horse thinks. In time they all love it.

Next, the **Piano Wire Release**

This exercise will release tension in the hind end, along the spine and all the way to the neck and chest muscles. I talk a lot about tension. We may not even notice it in our horses, but without routine maintenance like these exercises provide, it's there. It comes from work, worry, tack; it even comes from not working. Just like with us.

These exercises release both physical and mental tension, and strengthen the bond of trust between horse and human.

Stand beside the horse and gently work your fingertips in the center of the hind thigh muscle.

PIANO WIRE RELEASE

Search up and down, side to side until you find a cord-like tendon that runs up and down. When you find it, massage it up and down until you feel the release. Softening this tendon is huge. Remember to do both legs.

NOTE – Sometimes this is the first thing I do with a horse. Sometimes a horse is so tight on the front end from tension in the hind end they cannot relax or even lower their head, then I know I must do the Piano Wire first. You might remember this.

Next, the **Hip Circle Release**

This exercise will release and relax the hip, create balance and posture awareness, surefootedness and power.

Hold the fetlock and hock and gently rotate in small circles each way. And just as with the front leg, we want no movement in the hock, we want it in the hip.

HIP CIRCLE RELEASE

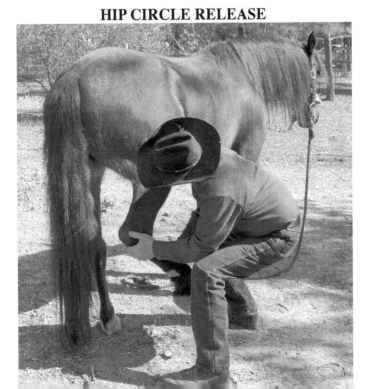

We want the hip to release. Keep her leg under her, not out to the side. While doing circles, move the leg slowly and gently upward, then work slowly down again and set the foot down on its toe behind the other foot.

NOTE – at first some horses are so tight that this exercise is very difficult, so be gentle and go only as far as she is comfortable, force nothing. Things will loosen up within a few days.

Next, the first motion and balance exercise, the **Rock Back**.

This exercise will teach correct posture, teach her to carry herself off her forehand and put the power and strength in the hind where it belongs.

First study your horse from the side as she stands ground tied. Look at her posture; learn to recognize the weight on her forehand, the angle of her chest and front legs. Then picture her standing with her weight shifted off her forehand. That is the position we are seeking.

Standing in front of your horse, very gently touch her shoulder point and say, "Rock Back."

ROCK BACK

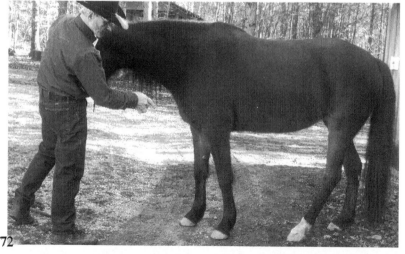

(Since most people ask their horse to back up this way, you need a verbal request that connects to this exercise; she will learn the two different verbal requests.) Be careful your body language does not tell her to step back. Be soft but secure in your stance, she will be looking to you to help her figure this out. We are looking for only a shift in posture and weight off the forehand, not a step back. If she steps back, start over. Watch for the slightest move, at first it may just be her pectoral muscle moving. Stop asking as soon as you see the slightest movement or change. You may need two inches of rock back to get her correct and off her forehand, and you may need to get it an eighth of an inch at a time.

Next, the **One-Step**

This exercise helps horses establish correct posture, patience, self-awareness and reconnects them to their feet.

Standing in front of your horse, say "One Step," and look for one complete step forward—that is, one front and one hind, then a pause, and ask for the Rock-Back. Allow her to feel the movement and the

ONE STEP

posture, then step back one step, the same feet, and Rock-Back. Repeat each side 3 or 4 times.

NOTE – Sometimes it is easier for the horse if you ask for the first step to be back rather than forward. Notice in the photo on the previous page Kessy has moved her left front and right hind. Keep the lead loose in your hand and your body soft. This is one exercise I do each and every time I tack up.

The final motion exercise for this series is the **Circle Tail Pull Leg Crossover**.

This exercise encourages hind end engagement and propulsion and self-awareness, relaxes the spine and releases the big rear muscles while creating surefootedness.

Ask your horse to "Walk On" in a slow easy circle on a 6-foot lead. Over the years I've been amazed at how many horses can't do that. That may be the first step in this exercise, teaching your horse to walk on, relaxed and easy in a circle. She'll also need to be comfortable with you taking her tail as she walks. While she is walking, grasp the tail and as the outside leg is lifting, tug gently on her tail to encourage her to cross over and set it down under her middle. Be quick on the release as soon as her foot touches down. Wait for the inside leg to move, then as the outside foot lifts, tug and release again. Do this for 3 to 5 circles, then switch sides. You'll need to keep moving with her, but maintaining the circle is important as well as a loose lead. It's all about softness, and relaxing ... Look closely at this picture and note the loose lead, Kessy is about to step down with her outside foot, not quite under her middle, but nice, and very important she is walking straight and upright while going in a circle. That's what you're looking for.

CIRCLE TAIL PULL CROSSOVER

That's all the exercises we'll discuss right now, and of course there are many more, but in my experience these are the best ones to maintain or restart a horse AND are the foundation for my "Therapy For Therapy Horses Exercises." In Pt 4 we'll talk about starting to ride and beginning conditioning or restarting under saddle.

Gitty Up ~ *Dutch Henry*

Restarting, Conditioning and Great Exercises For Your Horse Pt 4 (The Riding Part)

$$\bullet\!-\!\!-\!\!\langle\!\dot{\mathbf{\nwarrow}}\!\rangle\!-\!\!-\!\bullet$$

Howdy Friends,

I started this series when, with glee, I announced 2 weeks ago on Facebook I'd be riding again on September 1. I'd been sidelined 5 months with my cardiac adventure, and I briefly described my routine for getting my mare Kessy back in shape after our time off. A few friends asked what I do to restart a horse, so I figured it might make an interesting series.

This is the final installment of that 4-part series about restarting an idle horse. The first 3 parts discussed and demonstrated ground work exercises to release, relax and help create proper body carriage, posture and self awareness. The focus of this series is restarting a horse after time off, but these exercises are excellent any time, and I recommend them for every horse caregiver's routine. Many of them I do every time before I ride. Always. I do not believe in longeing as warm up; rather, I do these exercises.

Some folks say horses in big pastures or in track system Paddock Paradise type living don't need to be restarted. In my opinion that's wrong. They may not be as out of shape as a stalled or small lot kept horse, but they are not fit to ride any sort of time or distance, if we want to be fair, safe and healthy. Sure we may get away with just tossing on the saddle and tack and heading out for an hour or two ride after a horse has been idle a few months, but not only is it not fair, but the damage we do will eventually catch up with us... and our horse.

It's important for the health of your horse to get them back in shape for rides; a horse loses its cardio fitness in about 30 days, muscles about the same, and tendon and bone in about 90 days. I started Kessy's restart 2 weeks ago with the carrot stretches, and shared them on our Coffee Clutch blog. Then for the past 10 days I've done each of the exercises we've discussed in parts 1, 2 and 3 of this series once a day, exactly in the order I discussed them in this series. The entire routine takes Kessy and me about 30 minutes now. The first days it took about 40 minutes, for even though she has a Paddock Paradise, she was somewhat out of shape. I even found stiffness in her neck and hind legs, not really noticeable by just watching her, but by golly the exercises sure brought it to light. She improved quickly and by days 5 and 6 was close to back to her limber, balanced self, but even this morning she told me her hind legs were not yet perfectly released.

Imagine had I simply tossed on the saddle and went merrily along for an hour's ride, without the days of restart exercises, the stress it would have put on tight muscles and tendons. Sure she'd have done what I asked because she trusts me and is trained to, but she'd not have enjoyed it, and the discomfort would have chipped away at her trust and enthusiasm. I wonder how many horses are disciplined and sent for training, or sold, because their owners misunderstood their expressions of discomfort for bad behavior.

So now we're back in the in the saddle, and I'm taking in the world from the best seat God ever gave us. But we're still getting back in shape. Yea, me too, but I'm not the important one here. We start with 15-minute rides every day for about a week. Some folks say that's silly for a horse that was as fit as Kessy before her time off. But it's not. There is much that needs to happen in those first rides back. Think about all the areas the tack touches, the big muscles along the spine, the girth area, even the headstall, all are out of shape and need to come back. And every part of her needs to readjust to carrying weight—her back, legs, muscles, bones, heart, lungs, tendons and feet. And her vascular system. So 15 minutes a day for about a week, preferably on a trail so it's not in a ring always turning, is the first step. Oh and I reckon I should mention here, I'm not a fan of longeing for exercise or any reason, so that's why it's not part of our routine. Don't care for round pens either, but that's a subject for another day. And yes, I believe even show horses are better served on the trail than the ring. In fact I believe for every hour in the ring there should be two on the trail.

As I said, our first rides this week will be 15 to 20 minutes over the same course I walked for my cardio rehab. The following week we'll add time, about 10 minutes every other day, and mix in a little terrain change, and begin to ask for a little gaiting, about 3 to 5 minutes a time. The week after that we'll add more distance, a little more gaiting and more terrain change. By mid-week 4 we should be comfortably up to an hour with 15 to 20 minutes of gaiting. It takes about 30 days to get a horse minimally fit. When I trained for CTR and Endurance I learned it takes 60 days for cardio, 90 to 120 for muscle and a year for bone and tendon to condition.

All along I'll continue the exercises, and by the end of the month I can fine tune the exercises to the top-line exercises, pretty neck, the one step and rock back, which I do every time before I ride. I do the leg and circle pulls and the rest every now and then. Cool down, I'll do the top-line again.

So there you have it, the way I like to restart or simply maintain a horse. Of course there's a lot more, but I gotta go ride, and you've probably had all of me you can take. Kessy and I hope you enjoyed this little series, and will incorporate these great exercises into your daily routine.

Gitty Up ~ *Dutch Henry*

Finding the Release
(Not All Horses Tell You They are Hurting)

Howdy Friends,

While giving a horse a little therapy the other day, I was surprised by the amount of heat released when I started doing Tellington TTouch® circles across her back. This is a good little mare who always does what she's asked, even if she is a bit timid, so even though I could see before touching that there was plenty going on in her back, I was a still little surprised at the deep muscle soreness I found.

I rested my hands on the withers of the sweet little mare and examined her back. I saw a few problem areas and began to plan my approach. Sensing she was sorer than she was letting on, I started with tiny circles just behind her ears, so she might get used to this brand new feeling and touch. Even horses well cared for and handled gently and correctly, as this one is, take a few seconds to understand the new sensation of release the circles give, so it is important to start at a place that is not sore, giving plenty of time for the horse to understand and appreciate this new sensation.

As my fingertips floated in little circles from her ears down her neck toward her withers, she began to fidget and worry about me touching her back. Now this does two things: it distracts the horse's concentration, and it keeps her from enjoying the release from even the area not sore, so I knew I had to stop. Sensing her controlled but deep-seated worry about me touching her biggest "ouchy," I paused at her withers, laid my hands flat, and took a breath. I told her what I was about to do, and with my hands still resting on her,

I waited for her to accept them where they were. I rocked her ever so gently.

When she signaled with a softer eye, and big breath, that we might continue, I did. But, because she was so over-stimulated with worry about her back muscles, instead of using my fingertips, I used the flat of my hand for the first time over. That pleased her, and she began to go along with it. After a pass all along her back muscles to her rump, I gave her a few minutes to process, then repeated the whole thing again, using my fingertips.

It was then that I felt the big release of heat. It felt like the heat you'd feel holding your hand over a cup of hot coffee. The more I worked, the more heat came out. I've felt this before, even expect it sometimes, but still was surprised at it this time because the mare was so pleasant, and never showed signs of disagreement, or discomfort. I even asked the owner to feel the heat. The little mare softened and softened and we continued along through all the therapy exercises, and all went well.

I wanted to share this story because it is not uncommon for some horses to internalize their discomfort and just do their job. It is another reason I highly recommend these exercises to get to know the things you might miss about your horse's comfort.

Gitty Up ~ *Dutch Henry*

Section III

Understanding Your Horse

In this section, you'll find stories to both help and encourage you to understand your horse. These tales will help you understand the benefits of "putting the horse first" in everything you do, and slowing down and allowing your horse to guide you to a higher level of understanding.

It's For the Horse

Paradigm Shift

Expectations

Choices: Ours or Our Horse's?

There is More to Our Story

Horses and Post Traumatic Stress Disorder

It's for the Horse

Howdy Friends,

There are many different paradigms in the human and horse world. We are free to choose in which paradigm we place ourselves. Is our relationship with our horse based on what we want from it, and the expectations we place on our horse? Is our training for ourselves and our horse based on the outcome instead of the journey? Is our barn set up for our convenience or the horse's health and wellbeing, mentally and physically? Those are just a few thoughts and questions that constantly run through my mind.

Being a horse advocate, I have a little motto that guides my thinking and actions: "It's for the horse." When I write stories for Trail Blazer and Natural Horse magazines or my blog posts, and visit with friends in the wonderful world of Facebook, my thinking is always, "for the horse." I strive to point out that in all things, if the horse's point of view guides us, the outcome will be more glorious. More solid.

I remain amazed when people talk about their horses in the negative, and "demand" results, without taking time to appreciate the horse's perspective. Waiting for the horse to understand and process the training, or changing their own paradigm, seems to be a bother to far too many people, even today. Folks say they're going to "teach" their horse, or "train" their horse. I'd rather suggest "Learning together with their horse." No matter how many horses a person has known, every horse has more to teach "us," if we're willing to view things from the horse's perspective.

Barns are still today all too often built and maintained with the human interest as the guiding principle. It's easy to walk down a row of stalls to feed and care for the horses. What would the horse's perspective be about his housing?

Whether they are therapy horses, show horses, lesson horses and every other kind of discipline horses find themselves in, horses have a perspective of how they see their lives. Are they living it in a manner that makes sense to them? Is there something, perhaps a tiny thing, their human can do, or habit they can change, to help themselves see their own world through their horse's eyes?

How and what horses are fed can also be considered from the horse's point of view. Is it truly healthy for the horse, or convenient for the person?

If we follow the paradigm of "It's for the horse," a number of questions have their own answers.

Gitty Up ~ *Dutch Henry*

Paradigm Shift

Howdy Friends,

Tom stared at the pack of cookies on the fold-down tray as the train came out of the tunnel. Seemed like a good time to open the little bundle of black cookies with the creamy white filling that had been tempting him. Shifting in his seat, Tom was just about to reach for them when the gentleman beside him leaned forward, carefully opened the cellophane and pulled out a cookie.

"Who does he think he is, eating my cookie?" Tom made a point of being noticed as he tore the top off the tiny packet and snared two cookies. Without hesitation he stuffed them both in his mouth, and licked his fingers. The other fellow seemed unruffled, smiled and took two cookies, slowly eating one at a time as he looked out the window. Leaving a lone cookie in the pack, Tom let out an exaggerated sigh, snatched the last cookie, held it so the stranger could see, then devoured it in a single bite.

Satisfied he'd bested the cookie thief, Tom settled back in his seat prepared to silently gloat in his victory, and picked up the magazine on the tray in front of him. Then he saw it—another pack of cookies on the fold-down tray. He must have laid the magazine on top of them as he took his seat. Tom realized in that instant he had been the cookie thief, not the stranger beside him. He had been eating the other fellow's cookies all along! With a smile he moved the tiny pack of cookies to the center of the tray, gently tore the pack open and offered them to the stranger. This is what is known as a "Paradigm Shift."

I think this is a great little story to help us understand others better—family, friends, co-workers ... and our horses.

There's lots of talk in the horse industry nowadays about seeing things from your horse's point of view. I love that it has become fashionable to think of what your horse might need to understand, and what kind of brain your horse has—left, right, introvert, extrovert ... But how do you slow down enough to really see things from your horse's point of view? I've long held the thought that horses want to co-operate, not obey. Of course they will, and do, obey, but if that is how a person sees their horse, as something that must "obey," I don't think they can totally see the situation from the horse's point of view. Would you rather obey, or co-operate?

Our friend Tom on the train suddenly saw things from the stranger's point of view when he found his own pack of cookies hidden beneath the magazine. What a feeling of revelation, and perhaps embarrassment Tom must have felt in that instant. But now he could also see the first pack of cookies as the polite stranger had seen them, as something he'd been sharing. Not swiping, as Tom had thought he was doing when he viewed the situation from his own point of view.

It is not always easy to understand your horse's, spouse's, child's or friend's point of view, but if we slow down and listen with our whole brain and our whole heart, we just might hear a hint or two. It's called a Paradigm Shift, and it really works.

Gitty Up! ~ *Dutch Henry*

Expectations

Howdy Friends,

Do you approach your horse wearing your expectations on your sleeve? Sometimes it's hard not to, and in fact, sometimes it's the right thing to do. For without expectations there can be no results, right?

What if we think about our expectations from the horse's point of view? Would we see ourselves in a different light? Expectations to some are goals, to others dreams, to still others demands. Expectations, I think, are best when used as gentle guidelines.

It is wholly correct to expect our horses to be polite and respectful, as long as we are too. In our day-to-day relationship with our horses, many things go unsaid, they simply happen. Waiting politely to go through a gate, walking quietly beside us, standing while saddling, mounting, trimming hooves, these are routine and expectations that have become learned, practiced and ... expected. They are part of politeness.

There exists another world of expectations, those when we pursue our chosen activities with our horses. Things we need to learn together, whatever they may be—trail riding, showing, dressage, barrel racing— the things we might love to do may be the reason we love horses. There will be expectations as you learn to be a team together. Even if your horse did these things before you knew her, you'll both have expectations. If it is new to your horse, or you, you'll both have expectations.

Horses see, feel and hear expectations differently than we do. If we wear our expectations on our sleeve, our horse will see them as confusing demands. It will be difficult for her to relax and understand. When we allow our expectations to drive our thoughts and actions, the horse cannot feel the delicate, interwoven intricacies that make up the whole picture leading to the outcome we seek.

Our horses need us to keep our expectations as part of the whole, not the main focus. If we see our goal as part of the picture, and also see and feel the tiny steps required to get there, the picture we paint for our horse will be crystal clear. Our expectations will become theirs, too.

Gitty Up ~ *Dutch Henry*

Choices: Ours or Our Horse's?

—◦—‹✪›—◦—

Howdy Friends,

So much of what is done to, with and around horses is for the person's benefit, ease and perspective. It's natural and certainly correct for the person to choose the discipline, sport and activity they wish to engage in with their equine partner. That is, after all, why we have horses. To do stuff. And to do stuff we need to make choices. Many choices.

Choices about housing, feeding, health care, training, saddles, tack and much more. Almost every day there is a choice to be made about something.

Everyone is busy with life; families, living and jobs take lots of time. There is never enough money. Never enough time. So, many times the choices made by equine caregivers are made for reasons of human convenience, ease and dollars.

It most often takes no more time, or money, to make choices from the horse's perspective than from the human perspective. It requires only a simple paradigm shift. A brief pause to ask, "Am I doing this for my benefit, or my horse's?"

Housing is a big one that can easily be redirected to the horse's perspective. Instead of a claustrophobic stall or boring paddock, consider a "Paddock Paradise." These need not be overly large, but think about a playground of sorts, with trees, rocks, varied water and hay stations, fenced paths and rustic run-ins, to encourage walking about and engaging the horses' minds. Jaime Jackson wrote the best ever how-to book titled "Pasture Paradise," on bringing real nature into your horse's life. I highly recommend his easy to read and follow book. There's also an excellent Facebook page based on his book, where folks can interact and learn more from those who've done it.

Feeding is another easy change, and money saver too! A total forage diet is best, and most natural to a horse. In fact, craving grain is an acquired taste and habit for a horse, much like smoking is for humans. It is becoming increasingly understood that many of the health issues horses face stem from feeding processed feeds and grains. In a Pasture Paradise, using slow – feeder hay nets, secured at several different locations along the track, encourages movement and keeps the teeth, gut and mind busy all day. This one may add a bit of time to your day, but from your horse's perspective, it's worth it. Of course, hay should always be tested. Horses will require more hay on an all-forage diet, but in the slow-feeder nets, waste is negligible. Kessy weighs about 950 pounds and consumes about 25 pounds a day, more on cold days, for example. But I buy no grain, so really, it's less expensive.

How can I feed supplements with no grain? Easy, I use one pound of high quality timothy cubes soaked, and I mix in Kessy's enzymes and limited vitamins. Kessy hasn't had any grain in years. She will get a sprinkling of fresh vegetables. Minerals are fed free choice. Supplements should be fed sparingly, I think. There are a lot of things out there to take your money, and might have no benefit to your horse, and may build up toxicity, so be careful. If all the hay, and water, is tested, you'll know what your horse needs. And blood work is not hard to do if in doubt. I believe a horse's carriage, attitude, hair coat and hoof growth tell us a lot. Oh, and manure talks loudly too.

Everyone knows about my thoughts on going barefoot, so the only thing I'll say here is, not only is it best, but it'll save you money as well. And maintaining a horse's hooves is something you can learn to do yourself.

There are so many more choices equine caregivers must make: schooling, vaccinations, deworming, tack (would a horse ever chose to nail iron on their feet, have bits in their mouths, be prodded with spurs, contorted with tie-downs, martingales, tail sets and so many other tack-related choices?) and saddles, activity choices and on and on. If we chose to make these choices more from the horse's perspective than our own desires, I think we can be great stewards. In the long run it costs less too.

Gitty Up ~ *Dutch Henry*

There is More to Our Story

Howdy Folks,

With perked ears and sad eyes, Blackie watched as the truck drove away. Her long time friend, Chance called out in fear. Dust soon swallowed the trailer, but the whinnies continued. Frantically, Blackie raced along the board fence, head held over the top board, running as fast as her old legs could manage. She answered the calls with all the breath she had, and ran faster, ever faster, but soon the truck and the whinnies were gone. Straining over the fence she looked far away, far into the setting sun where her friend had gone. Blackie stood well into the night, searching the horizon for her friend's return. Deep inside she knew that would not happen. There would be hay at the barn, there always was, but tonight she would eat no hay.

In her many years Blackie had watched other friends leave. Too many. Sometimes it was she who was taken away. The first time, she was running free with her mama, and the others. She hardly remembers her mama, but she remembers that horrid, hot, terrifying day. It started like any other, scampering about playing with the other young ones. Then the run came! Chased from all sides, there was yelling, panic and pain. Blackie still feels the pain in her feet and her chest from running so many miles trying so hard to keep up. Her legs were too short, she lost sight of mama, and she cried out. Like today, trying to run and call at the same time.

She never saw her mama after that day. Or her other friends. It had been her first ride in a crowded truck. Tonight, looking over the fence for Chance, she remembered that first ride. A long ride, she remembers how thirsty she'd become. How tired. Where is mama? She'd cried out as long as she had voice.

The ride took her to a place so different from before. She'd never been inside, the air was tight, smelled and felt strange, and there was so much noise. She had her first lessons there, human lessons. It was hard, at first, to understand humans, but after a while she learned to accept them. Even love some of them. For a while she played there, outside with new friends. Frolicking in the big fields was almost like being home again. It was there she was taught many new things, human things. Some were fun, some confusing, but she always tried her best. In the evenings she and her new friends would gather together, groom each other and help each other understand. Blackie was different from the others, they had all been born right there. They seemed to learn faster than she, but the friendships they forged were just as real as the friends she'd left behind, before the big chase.

She walked from the fence, just far enough so she could lie down. If the truck and Chance came back, she would be right here, waiting.

It had been a long time since Blackie had thought of those early friends, but tonight she remembered each of them. That first summer, long ago, in the new place, had seen each of them leave, one at a time. Blackie stayed two more years. She had her first foal there. Those sweet months with her baby by her side, those are some of her fondest memories. She would have two more foals, each at new places. Each one she left behind as she was taken to new places.

Blackie rolled onto her side, stretched out her neck, heaved a heavy sigh. She thought of those babies. She wondered where they were tonight.

She pulled her tired legs under her, stood and shook. It always feels good to shake. She gave another look far away, and got lost in her thoughts. She thought of the places she'd lived. She remembered the friends she'd made along the way. She thought of the children so proud to ride her. For a wonderful few years she'd been proud to teach children to ride at the beautiful farm in the mountains. Those were fun days, and she'd had great friends there. Horses and human. She met Chance there. Chance told her his stories. She told Chance her stories. They understood each other.

One day, she and Chance were loaded together, and they came here. For a while they taught children to ride here too. Then no more children came and it was just she and Chance, and Michelle. Michelle was nice, perhaps the kindest of all the people she'd known. There had been some bad places, and people, over the years, but here with Michelle things were very good. It was peaceful here.

She would miss Chance; she knew he would miss her. Perhaps he'll go to a place where there is a woman like Michelle, who can hear him. And know there is more to his story. There is always more to our stories, and we can tell them, if people listen. Blackie laid down, stretched out, and closed her eyes.

Gitty Up ~ *Dutch Henry*

Horses and Post-Traumatic Stress Disorder

---◦❖◦---

Howdy Friends,

We are all very sensitive to people enduring Post-Traumatic Stress Disorder (PTSD)—veterans, first responders, police officers and, of course, women and children. But what about horses? Can horses suffer from PTSD? I submit they can and, in fact do, all too often. Sadly, this is usually diagnosed as bad or incompliant behavior and a wide variety of "training" routines are administered, most of which can only deepen the grip of PTSD in the suffering horse.

PTSD occurs when a traumatic or sustained stressful event or events occur, causing an overactive adrenaline response that creates deep neurological patterns in the brain. These can persist for decades after the event or events that triggered the fear. These patterns in the brain are a transformation making the person hypersensitive to future stressful or fearful events, real or perceived.

Some of our Coffee Clutch and Facebook friends know bits and pieces of my childhood, the unspeakable abuse I endured for over three years locked in that room. I can tell you, to this day as an old geezer in his 6th decade of wandering this beautiful world, it takes only a single instance of the wrong kind of fear or stress and I'm 8 years old again, back in that horrid room with the blackened window. Interestingly, recent studies at Harvard Medical School found that adults who were in foster care for one year between the ages of 14 and 18 were found to have higher rates of PTSD than combat veterans, and the recovery rate was significantly lower.

I share the tidbit of my personal struggles to help make the point: the younger the individual when the original trigger events occur, the more ingrained the PTSD and the more difficult the personal battle becomes to manage it. It walks with you as an unwelcome friend every day. Unexplainable, or out of context behavior, feelings and emotions simply occur without the ability to completely manage or control. They are as much a part of PTSD as kisses and handholding are to love.

In my travels I've seen many horses, young, old and middle-aged, displaying the symptoms of deeply ingrained PTSD. I know I'm right about this, and it breaks my heart. They may not have all been abused, they may have been weaned too young, trained too hard too young, trained, owned or shown by one, or too many individuals who could not understand them and disciplined instead of trying to connect with and understand them. They may have been yanked from friendships or homes in ways they could never understand.

How can we help horses with PTSD? Our interactions, our intent, our training should follow one simple rule: "Ignore the negative and celebrate the positive." And in everything we do, operate from the horse's perspective ... We want to do our best to never be the trigger that drives them back into that horrid room with the blackened window.

Gitty Up ~ *Dutch Henry*

SECTION IV

Building Trust and Confidence

Trust is the most important thing we need to build between ourselves and our equine partners—or any partner, for that matter. Trust and confidence are tied together. The stories in this section talk about building and creating a deeply trusting partnership, a trust with its foundation rooted in confidence.

Consistency Builds Confidence

H owdy Folks,

Horses build confidence by getting it right, not by being corrected. My mentor, Diane Sept, teaches we should "Conduct ourselves in a manner that commands respect." That of course does not suggest you "boss" your horse around. In fact, it proposes you hold yourself in a manner that can be counted on to be reliable, consistent. Just as we appreciate certain boundaries, guidelines or structure and familiar procedures, so do horses. Even if you study the wild horses, you'll see they have their routines that vary little. And on a more humorous note, look at your own pastures or paddocks and you'll see the routes they take are well worn paths. They are comfortable, confident knowing what, where, when and how. So are we.

So we should take that basic tenet in confidence building and apply it to our relationship with our horses. The little things we do each time we interact with our horse should be consistent. It's not fair to the horse for a person to sometimes act one way and other times act differently. It only causes confusion for the horse and will prevent confidence from taking root. Varying behavior and posture by the person will cause the horse to make mistakes while trying to guess what is expected of them, for which the person may be inclined to discipline. And discipline chips away at confidence.

We've all seen folks jerk the lead rope and yell at their horse for stepping on their feet, or rubbing, stopping or any number of things. What if every time that horse had been led anywhere the person acted exactly the same way and the horse had the confidence to know what was expected of her, and no discipline was necessary. I'll also suggest here that if a horse steps on a person's feet, it might be the person who needs the discipline, not the horse.

Consistency builds confidence. If every time a horse is led through a gate she is asked to stand and wait quietly, and once through the gate is gently turned back to face the gate, asked to lower her head to remove the halter, then released, she will know what to expect every step of the way, and will never need discipline. If the person sometimes allows the horse to dance through the gate, hold her head high and step about while removing the halter, and other times is expected to "behave," the horse will be confused, and worry about what comes next. And most likely the person will feel the urge to "discipline," which further chips away at confidence.

That little example should follow through in everything we do with our horses. The way we approach learning new things together should always be the same. Allow the horse the time she needs to make sense of the new adventure, maneuver or challenge. Celebrate and build on the positive, ignore the negative and the negative will go away.

Confidence is very important to a horse—and thus, to your relationship. And consistency builds confidence.

Gitty Up ~ *Dutch Henry*

Building a Horse's Confidence
And Building Fictional Characters

Howdy Friends,

Let's see if I can tie two emails that are worlds apart (are they really?) together. One is a horse question, the other is about writing. A Facebook friend emailed and asked how I build confidence in a horse. Another Facebook friend asked how I build a character in a story. Both emails used the word "build," and they came within five minutes of each other!

The writing question came first so ... When I'm thinking of creating a character, at first of course I'll need to establish gender. Maybe. But I don't really care about any other physical characteristics, unless something jumps out and yells at me, "Hey I'm tall and very athletic." I might store that for future references. But mostly I'll address the physical characteristics as the story unfolds. I may set the stage with a brief hint such as "With a delicate, quivering hand, she flipped open her phone, gazed at the tiny screen and carefully considered her next move."

I've never been real big on a horse's conformation, either. I see a horse from within. I believe every horse can perform at the highest level her body will allow. It's our responsibility to make that possible. So I guess, as with my fictional characters, I don't really care that much about physical characteristics of horses either. We can address them as need be, as we go along. The first thing I might do with a horse who lacks confidence is ask for her to take a single step forward or back. I'll store how she took that step in my mind for future reference.

After I establish in my mind my fictional character is tall, athletic and worried, I can paint a bigger picture. I look at the whole scene, like a painting on the wall. But I notice the little things in the picture. The big things will always take care of themselves, if you address the little things, such as how she enters a room boldly with long strides, but fidgets with her hands and dislikes eye contact during tense conversations. I can use these later when I need to add tension, or slow the reader down.

I notice the little things about a horse's confidence. How does she stand, walk, hold her head? How does she respond to requests? Does she focus on me, or look far away? Just as in creating a character, I'll keep them in mind as we move ahead into her story. I can use these foundations to build her confidence.

Now that I've laid the groundwork for my character, I can move ahead in the story and continue to add layer upon layer as I write the scenes in which she interacts with other characters or tackles situations, or thoughts, on her own. As I build the character I can always go back to the basics the reader already knows. She's tall, can be bold, but can be nervous, is athletic and thinks deeply. It's important, as I continue building the character, to keep the basics in mind to fall back on in times of impact or excitement. It's important to the reader to have characters they can rely on. Fundamentals matter.

When building a horse's confidence, after I've noticed her basic characteristics, thought process, what she's worried about, things she can tolerate and most importantly, things she really enjoys and looks forward to, I can begin building her confidence, one layer at a time. I do this by spending a lot of time asking her to do the things she already has a liking for, and the confidence to be able to handle them. As we work together, adding layer upon layer of confidence by adding new challenges, I'll keep going back to those basics she understands and enjoys. Those basics are the foundation on which all else is built. They are the things the horse can rely on.

So there you have it, I guess ... Whether I'm building a fictional character for a novel or building confidence in a horse, it's a matter of seeing the solid foundation and carefully adding layers until I have the picture I see in my mind established for the reader, or the horse. One little step at a time.

Gitty Up ~ *Dutch Henry*

Earning the Trust Your Horse
Wants to Give

———————⟨✲⟩———————

Howdy Friends,

Over the years I've known more than a few horses,
loved some deeply. My mare Kessy took a long time
to accept and offer trust, and love. She will always
maintain her strong-willed independence; it's a huge
part of her—that part that made her so easy to be
misunderstood. She uses her powerful independence
now to offer a loving, caring bond. And I accept it
with joy in my heart.

That deep trust can only be earned; in Kessy's case,
it took years. Oh, she dialed in rather quickly, but
the deep trust took years, and our bond continues to
strengthen. She has been, and continues to be, one of
my finest teachers.

We've been partners now for nearly 5 years, and
before we met, her independent nature had caused
her to be handled in a way that chipped away at her
ability to find trust easy to give. She had developed a
strong personality of resistance, defense and defiance.
Not because she was mean or stubborn and liked
to bite and "snake" at people, but because she was
misunderstood. It took 6 months for Kessy to accept a
hug. Six more months for her to give a hug back.

I learned, and adopted, from my mentor, Diane Sept,
a philosophy that works every time it's employed:
"Ignore the negative and celebrate the positive." It
works like magic, not as quickly as magic, but just as
completely.

Gaining the trust of a horse can happen quickly, or
as in Kessy's case, take a long time. All it takes is
respect, and not asking for things they are not ready

for, can't do, or are afraid to do. In everything we must offer respect, trust and confidence. Then that list of not ready fors, can't dos and afraid ofs gets shorter and shorter. The list of Can and Will do grows longer. Trust becomes deeper as confidence builds.

It also takes awareness on our part—awareness of our horse's limits, worries and attitude. I believe it is wrong to push a horse beyond her comfort zone. That to me is not trustbuilding. I believe we must understand their limits and stop short of them, relieve the pressure; then the next time that limit will be stretched further—by the horse, not the human. That builds trust. A trust she can count on to be there.

Sometimes we hear advice such as "Push them through it." I'd rather give them the confidence to build up to getting through it on their own. Sure, anyone can "make" a horse do something, but to build trust we need to invite them, and allow for time to build trust, in us and themselves.

Another piece of advice I find hard to take is "You can't let them win." I find that especially offensive. Win what? Usually that advice is thought to be useful when things are going wrong, the horse is thought to be disobeying, refusing, acting up, when almost always they are either not ready for what is being asked of them, are confused or afraid. In those cases I like to stop, let her relax; perhaps visit something she is totally confident in doing so she can feel the joy of accomplishment. Revisit the challenging thing another day, but ask for less.

Asking ourselves every step of the way ... "How does my horse see this thing I want, as a demand or a request? Am I building confidence and trust? Am I celebrating the positive?" Our goal is to build trust she can count on and wants to give.

Gitty Up ~ *Dutch Henry*

I Can Get Lost in the Little Things

Howdy Friends,

My inbox has links to interesting articles, blogs and newsletters stacked up in it each morning, and throughout the day. I try hard to at least study the headlines, and like most of us, I'd surely never have the time to read them all, but even a headline and first few sentences browsing often offers a wealth of information.

There was one worthy of note this morning that, although aimed at authors and how they might best engage their audience, keep them interested, create energy and have their audience eager for more, reading it caused me to think our relationship with our horses. The article points out how most authors do the things they are obligated to do, and feel too strapped for time to do the extra things they should do to engage and build a report with their audience.

The author suggests a series of little things, like Twitter, Facebook and Blogs where you actually reply to, and engage your audience with more than the basics of what book you're writing now and where you'll be at book signings, but talk to them about their interests and goals and other fun stuff. Things that make an author's audience eager to hear from him or her.

Well, of course my mind went to the relationship between a horse and her person. There is an old saying in the sales world, "People don't care about how much you know until they know how much you care." That applies to how your horse sees you, too.

For a horse/human relationship to flourish, it takes a lot more than the basic care needs being fulfilled—the things we are "obligated" to do. More than housing, feed, water, health care and training. Remember, your horse won't really care, unless she knows you do. Sure she'll learn the skills you're asking for, but to excel and glow, it takes a lot of little things. Horses are social. They yearn for a connection. For me, I've never bought into the whole predator/prey thing or the alpha mare thing, or teach them who's in charge ... What is that?! ... I don't care about that stuff ... whatever horse I've worked with, I've always felt we were equals. I treat people the same way. In fact, I go a step further and am happy to take advice from any horse I'm working with, or person, and see where it goes. But I like to pay attention to the little things. I can get lost in the little things.

Horses, like an author's audience, will become disinterested if all they ever get is the things you are "obligated" to give them. Think about that. How would you feel if the only time you saw your human was at feeding time, and if the horse is boarded not even then, or when you were being groomed for a show, or trained for this or that.

It's the little things that build love, trust and willingness. That's why I'm such a huge fan of Tellington TTouch® and Connected Groundwork®. With tiny little things you can show your horse you care. Have coffee with your horse. Take them on walks, not under saddle. Answer their TWEETS with real answers, not just an obligated response. Laugh with them when things get silly, don't scold them. Spend time with them when you are expecting nothing of them, except being together. Remember, training to a horse is what SHE feels "obligated" to do ... Join her in the things she does for fun.

Think about this ... How many times have you heard from friends, or maybe experienced it yourself, that after a horse has had a serious injury or illness and was nursed back to health by their person for weeks or months, they enjoy a totally new relationship. Like something they could never have imagined. It was the giving, without asking for anything that melded those hearts. Think of rescue horses and the bonding there.

When your horse knows how much you care, whatever you want to do together will happen ... Just like magic.

Gitty Up ~ *Dutch Henry*

It's About Who They Are,
Not What They Are

Howdy Friends,

Writing, people and horses always seem to go
together for me. One of the novels I'm working
on, "Coming Home," opens with the scene of the
protagonist, Billie, sitting at the end of her parents'
farm lane, pausing, thinking just a moment before
driving in. We visit reuniting with family, and an
old friend drops by too. Midway through the first
chapter, in a scene set in a diner, Billie learns there's
big trouble, and tension builds quickly. Now modern,
conventional wisdom has it that everything prior to
the diner scene should be cut, and the story should
start with the "action, or tension."

Today everyone wants to start with the "action." You
even see it in the current movies and TV shows that
start with explosive action, then drift into flashbacks.
How many times have we seen "Three days earlier"
on the screen, or in a book? Sure, the action might
be gripping, but if you think about it, it's action for
action's sake. It's rarely compelling, so the writer
needs to "take you back," so you can get to know and
feel for the characters. And truly care about them.

I like to do things a little differently. Publishers,
editors and agents tell us, "If you start your story with
reflection, contemplation or a character pondering,
it will not be published." Or read. I took that advice
when my novel "We'll Have The Summer" was
published, and I will forever regret the readers never
saw the opening paragraphs that were cut to "start
with the action." The readers missed out on tender,

precious thoughts Mary Holt had looking out the kitchen window above the sink. Oh sure, I tried to weave those emotions in later, but the reader would have known who Mary was in the first paragraph on a deeper level.

I agree a story can't start with a ton of baggage, or backstory. But I also believe that the need to start with tension, action, momentum is somehow a sign of our over-stimulated time. To me it feels like too often it's about the "what," not the "who." And the "who" is important.

In fact, I believe that "who" is much more important than "what." In a story, in life, with our horses. I believe when working with our horses, it is far more important to get to know "who" they are before we begin to "train" them. That's another word I'm not too fond of—"training." Better than some of the other words used, but still very much in the world of "what" instead of "who."

If we take the time to allow our horses to tell their story, if we listen to their opening paragraphs of reflection and contemplation, we will know them more deeply. That will allow us to have an understanding of "who" they are instead of "what" they are, which will make possible a deeper, richer form of communication that makes sense to both the horse and the human.

To me, making the time to learn who a person, character in a novel or a horse is—is time well spent. It's the fundamental building stone for everything that follows. It's about who they are, not what they are.

Gitty Up ~ *Dutch Henry*

Get Even? Or Build Confidence?

—◆——⟨✵⟩——◆—

Howdy Friends,

It's not always okay to speak up, I really do understand that. And I practice that. Most of the time. However, there are times when choosing not to speak up leaves us with inner thoughts and internal conversations wrestling to understand.

The other day I was at a feed store, and while browsing the shelves I overheard a young woman complaining about her horse turning around on the trail. Her friend promptly suggested, "Oh yea, when a horse does that you just keep him turning, around and around, let him know that it's more work to turn around than to do what you want," or words to that effect. I thought about countering that suggestion, but who am I? I'm certainly no trainer. I do alright helping folks learn how to make their horses feel better with exercises, but a trainer I'm not. So I just did my business and moved along.

But I never understood, or subscribed to that method of "training." First that kind of turning around and around can, and often does, cause the horse to become heavy on the forehand. Which is counterproductive to opening a horse's mind, as a horse on its forehand is most likely to be in flight mode, and that's not really a thinking place. Second, causing a horse to become heavy on its forehand is exactly opposite of correct and healthy body posture and carriage. Lastly it just feels and sounds wrong.

To me that kind of approach always just felt like … "Getting even." … As if to say, "You wanna do that, I'll show you what that gets you." Different approaches for different folks, I reckon ... But to me, "teaching a horse a lesson" falls far short of "teaching a horse to be confident."

What do I do in a case where my horse refuses, or rebels? ... Depends. But it's never, ever a "get evenism." When Kessy, early in our relationship, refused to go down the trail, I dismounted and led her. In those early days, I did a lot of walking, and walking for me is difficult. But you see, each little step helped her gain confidence. I'd walk a little, find a spot I could sit down and let her pick at the grass if there was any, or just take in the moment being out there together. We did this for weeks. Eventually she gained the confidence to go happily down the trail. And today goes alone on any trail, anywhere. I also have used that technique on many of the horses I helped to rehabilitate. Just sit, give them time to think and adjust ... works every time it's tried.

This confidence can then be transformed to other challenges. That's where I feel, and it's only my opinion, "getting even, or teaching them a lesson" leaves the horse wanting. Those do not build confidence. Without confidence, the horse cannot truly enjoy or look forward to doing things with you. Sure she might perform, but it'll remain an effort. Not be a joy. And it's difficult to build on.

I contend, when a person expects a horse to "obey," they are not "hearing" the horse. When you help your horse build confidence, cooperation is freely given. A horse who has been trained to "obey" will too often see your requests as just another thing they "Must Do." A horse who has been allowed to learn by building confidence will see your requests as adventures. A side benefit will be a horse who has less separation anxiety, and will be with you on the trail, even when other horses around her are worried and anxious. It's a confidence thing.

Gitty Up ~ *Dutch Henry*

What About Horses' Emotions?

◆——◆◇◆——◆

Howdy Friends,

I'm often asked about how I feel about horses' emotions. Surely horses don't have emotions on the same level as humans, some folks say. Some say to try to project human emotions on horses is folly, foolish. Some say we simply want to believe horses feel emotions like we do. Some folks don't even think about it.

Are emotions the same as caring, connection, bonding or even the ever-popular "Join Up®"? I believe you can't have any of those without emotion, and we all know our horses care about us, bond with us, and yes, join up with us.

What about respect? Some will ask. To gain respect from a horse, we must first give it. Isn't that the same as with our human peers?

What about love? Can they love us the same as a person can love us? What would be so wrong about accepting and believing that a horse can love a human as deeply as they can another horse, or we can another human? When I'm away for a few days doing clinics, Kessy nickers and loves on me when I get back like crazy. Robbie says if I'm gone more than two days, she even gets pouty. Usually I want to get right into the house to Robbie as soon as I park our geriatric Tahoe, but Kessy will carry on so much I often need to hug her first! Then she'll follow me right to the back door!

Oh, most folks say they're just acting that way because they're trained, or looking to you for food, or any other of the many standard explanations of how horses act and react.

Emotions play a huge part in any relationship—human-to-human or horse-to-human. In relationships with my horses over the years, I not only considered what they required when learning new things but also their emotions while learning, too. In the time I've spent rehabilitating horses, I noticed a wide range of emotions – from fear, to mistrust, to need, to shut down, to confusion, to seeking advice and leadership. Building their confidence meant understanding their emotions on a level equal to mine. And it meant seeing them as equals. I really dislike the "You gotta be in charge" theme. If we're equals, we can achieve cooperation, support, loyalty and love. In true partnerships. Partners do things for each other because they want to, not because they're "trained" to … I see Kessy as my equal.

I'm not a trainer, but in all things I believe love, honor, respect and understanding and feeling emotions make any relationship strong, lasting and sterling. Including a relationship with horses. Sure, training is important, of course. But I submit understanding and honoring the emotions of the horse makes training smoother and more lasting. And actually I'm not even fond of the word "training." I like education or teaching better.

In my heart, I believe if a lot more folks projected human emotions on horses … a lot fewer horses would suffer.

So go ahead, project your emotions onto your horse, and remember to let hers touch your heart and guide your hand as you teach, and learn too.

Gitty Up ~ *Dutch Henry*

What's in the Spirit of Your Horse's Nickname—Or Any Word?

Howdy Friends,

What's in a name? Not a new question to be sure, but a good one. It's often been asked, and will certainly be asked many more times. Names serve many purposes, but my thoughts today are about nicknames, sometimes called, "pet names."

When I'm at the feed store, tack shop, therapeutic riding centers, other barns or just reading emails and Facebook posts, I hear the strangest things. Often I'm compelled to ponder what I hear. I wonder sometimes if people "hear" themselves. I had a sentence in my novel when Mary asks herself, "Did he hear what he just said?" Referring to the doctor's comment inviting her to take the thirsty violet in the hospital room home with her. "You take it Mary, it'll just die here." He had just given her the news her cancer had returned.

Recently I was at a barn for a clinic, and a woman introduced her horse to me. "I call him Blockhead," she told me with a smile. It's not the first time I winced at a horse's negative nickname. I've heard most of them by now. It always sets me back a step, though. And hopefully always will. I'm pretty sure I'll never really understand why some folks genuinely believe it's cute to use an insulting nickname for their horse. It's fun to sound cute and witty, I understand. What I don't understand is why so often the cute and witty is rooted in the negative.

Pause a second here, take a breath and feel the difference between "Blockhead" … and … "Handsome." One feels uninviting, harsh and paints pictures in your head of stubbornness, adversity. The other feels warm, receiving, paints pictures in your head of someone you admire, want to be with. Which would you rather be called? Which would you be happiest to respond to? Which would make you more willing to be a partner?

We all claim to understand, here in the horse world, that horses sense our emotions, even our thoughts. Yet somehow folks expect a disconnect from that understanding to the nickname given their horse. And it's even more than that. The words we say trigger emotions and feelings within ourselves too. So even though we may want to use the moniker "Blockhead" in an endearing way, it'll always release a different kind of energy than "Handsome." That energy will be perceived by your horse. And yourself.

Remember the old saying "Sticks and stones can break my bones but names can never hurt me?" Not true, is it? I submit the very reason that old jingle was given birth was to try to hide the hurt the names can deliver.

Nature does not like negative. Nature runs from negative. Negative causes imbalance in nature. You may feel that simply using a negative word in a cute way to name your horse makes a difference, but the words set about a different energy in your own body. Words truly do mean things, and while we may try to alter their meaning, beneath and within the word lies the energy of it—positive or negative.

One of the most remarkable examples of this is the work done by Masaro Emoto with ice crystals. He has published several books discussing and illustrating the "Messages In Water." Emoto spent years freezing water to examine the crystals. His work, both celebrated and criticized, showed that water exposed to kind words froze into beautiful geometrical crystals while water exposed to unkind words froze into distorted and randomly formed crystals. I'm one of those who celebrate his work.

I also wonder about the distant thoughts connected with negative nicknames. When we think of our horse from the house or when we're at work, their name on our mind creates an energy. It can be a dance, or a standoff. Or confused energy. How we picture our horse, our relationship, our bond, is affected by the name. Is it a joke, a put down, or a compliment, a sign of affection?

The energy you send, and receive is in direct relationship to your thoughts. Have you ever gone to a meeting and as you stood outside the door, just about to enter, your thoughts are racing, you feel excited, or maybe you're worried. Maybe you're bouncing off the walls happy. Your energy is already ahead of you in that room mixing with the energy and emotions in there. You're picking up on the energy coming back to you. Everyone has felt this.

Perhaps you've felt it and brushed it off as just your worry, apprehension or excited anticipation. Of course there is some of that, but the energy from within you flows out from you and receives energy too. That energy is in tune with your thoughts. I believe it can't help but to be that way.

So back to your horse's nickname. When you think of her from afar, would you like to send thoughts from a name whose negative energy must be overcome? Wouldn't you rather send happy energy and thoughts? As you approach or introduce her to folk, don't you want to think thoughts of happy and partnership?

Kessy and I hope you'll spread the word about the spirit in your horse's nickname. Kessy's name, you ask? Kessy is my nickname for Keziah, the name of Job's second beautiful daughter.

Gitty Up ~ *Dutch Henry*

Why Horses (And People) Trust Some People and Doubt Others

Howdy Friends,

Did you ever notice how some horses just seem to read their person's mind? How they seem to always be on the same page? A solid, dependable team? Did you wonder about, perhaps get a little envious, surely curious, as to how that can be? It has a lot to do with consistency, but it has a lot to do with a person's emotional stability too. Which I reckon is a big part of constancy.

It also has a lot to do with the person's self-confidence and the ability to respectfully display that self-confidence. Horses (and people too) want teammates, partners and friends they can count on to be there for them. To lead them, hear them, consider their point of view. And yes, horses each have their own point of view and it can, and will, meld with ours. They key is to be confident enough to look and listen for it. Not to correct or discipline, but rather to support, guide, teach and empower.

I'm all for praising a horse's misstep, wrong move or confusion. The key is to praise and support the attempt, no matter how tiny—not correct the misstep or wrong move. Go with the mistake, see where it leads. Then try again. Improvements leading to perfection come far sooner with mountains of praise than with buckets of corrections and discipline. Take the mistake, or miscue and redo the exercise or movement seeking improvement in baby steps along the way.

My mentor, Diane Sept, used to say, "Carry yourself in a way that commands respect." I like to add, "And be sure you give it too, in the form of praise."

Praise for a horse (or person) can be a big deal. "GOOD GIRL!" and a pat on the neck speak volumes. Or it can be a simple, quiet acknowledgement of a job, task or cooperation well done. If you listen, your horse will tell you which she needs.

Self-confidence and emotional stability mean you'll be consistently supportive. You won't "fly off the handle" and scold, correct harshly, intimidate and confuse your horse ... How can a horse become soft, trusting, truly cooperative, if they must always be on guard for the next explosion of discipline. I actually believe it is never okay to discipline a horse ... well, never with a few exceptions related to safety and health. Self-confident instruction based upon solid respectful teamwork and cooperation will always build a solid relationship of trust. Every time.

Let's look at stepping into the saddle. I'll use my mare Kessy as an example. When we first partnered, she would not even come within five feet of the mounting block. If she did, she wasn't going to stand to mount. (Of course you must first be absolutely certain there is no physical reason she can't stand still.) I had to think of how I could help her understand this really mattered to me. Back then I could still mount from a two-step block, so I set it next to the barn wall allowing just enough room for her to stand, and we started mounting that way. If she moved forward, I would simply lead her around without a word, and stand her next to the block again. When she was in the correct position, I would ask her to "Stand." After mounting I'd give her a bit of carrot. (Still do, it's a kind of flexion exercise.) We did this for a while, then eventually I moved the block away from the wall, and it no longer mattered where, or how we mounted. She just needed that little bit of guidance and support the barn wall offered her as she was making sense of the mounting deal. Today, she'll not move a hoof until I ask her to "Walk on." Never once did I scold, yank on the reins or demand she "Stand Still!" We've all seen that, right?

As time went on, it became necessary for me to mount and dismount from a platform, and it's quite an ordeal some days. She stands like a concrete statue as I clamber aboard. It's a confidence built of trust, and that trust builds a desire to not only cooperate but also to be there for me. Kessy knows I'll not let my emotions take over and yell at her when she gets things a bit wrong. She knows I'll support her just as she supports me.

I'll take it a bit further. I have bad health days and not so bad health days. Kessy knows the difference. She's always beyond perfect for mounting and dismounting, tacking, grooming, hoof care, all ground tied, but once we're on the trail, she either treads along gently and slowly, or as is her core nature, frolics and announces her attitude—depending upon my ability that day to sit the saddle. This cooperation and connection is born of a bond built on trust, not discipline.

The secret to those horses who seem to be able to read their person's mind? I believe it's as simple as being able to trust their person to be both emotionally balanced and consistent. And respectful.

Gitty Up ~ *Dutch Henry*, and *Kessy* too.

SECTION V

Horse Care

Stories in this section will discuss housing, feeding, healthcare, hoof care and all things for the horse's physical wellbeing, which of course cannot really be separated from the horse's mental wellbeing. My belief is to keep it as natural and holistic as possible. My column in Natural Horse Magazine is called "Holistic Hall of Fame," and that may give you a hint about my beliefs. These stories are offered as my point of view, as a horse lover, advocate and admirer—not as a clinician, veterinarian or specialist of any kind.

Practices For a Healthy, Happy Horse

Howdy Friends,

Horses will get along, as many of them prove over and over again, with less than ideal conditions and treatment, but that does not mean they are happy, healthy or thriving. In my opinion, we owe it to our horses to provide for them with as natural a lifestyle as we can possibly provide. Each of us as owners or caregivers have limitations placed on us by such things as economics, lifestyle, jobs, property, riding disciplines and more. Our efforts must be to do the best we can within our own circumstances for the physical and mental health of our horses.

Basically we could sum up a lot of the healthy, happy needs for our horses in one sentence. "No shoes, no stalls, no grain, limited grass and seeing everything from the horse's point of view." That's pretty much my focus; to me, those are the most important things to the secret of a happy, healthy horse.

No shoes. Friends who've been following me here on our Coffee Clutch, or on Facebook, already know I'm adamant that all horses can go barefoot—and will be healthier for it. All the arguments against it, to me, fall short, and lie in the camp of seeing it from the human's perspectives, not the horse's. Of course a few things must be done differently, and that may take more effort than some are willing to devote.

No stalls. This includes no stalls with small paddocks or pastures. The only time a horse should be confined to a stall is illness, traveling (shows, performances, horse camping, etc.) or other special short-time circumstances. Even if space to roam is an issue, the Paddock Paradise or track system can turn an unhealthy half-acre paddock or unwholesome 2 to 5 acre toxic lush grass pasture, into a playground for health and contentment. This only takes a little effort to set up, and then it's there forever, and can be constructed anywhere, even with limited funds.

No grain. That's it, simple. Horses are designed to be forage eaters. Grain and today's high potency grasses do bad things to the insides, and the attitudes, of a horse. Again they can deal with it, but these things will eventually take their toll. Don't you think it's odd the epidemic of ulcers? Slow-feeder hay nets positioned at several locations offering low sugar hay around the clock, will promote movement, health and clear headedness conducive to solid relationships, health and happiness.

Limited grass. We've touched on this, but typical pastures filled with lush grass or patches of grass mixed in weeds are as toxic to horses as fast food and overstuffed couches in front of televisions are to humans. Again, make it your mission to have horses under your care thriving in a track system. Horses, even in big pastures with other horses, move about 5 miles a day, or less. Horses in the wild move 20 and more miles a day. Horses benefiting from a track system mimic the movement of wild horses. Health benefits are seen within weeks of making the change.

Seeing things from the horse's perspective. Housing, feeding, riding, training, everything ... the horse must come first. When that drives every thought and action of a horse owner or caregiver, things take a paradigm shift toward a healthy, happy horse. When that shift occurs, everything becomes easier, no matter the discipline the horse and human play in. I see having a horse as a part of my life as a privilege, and every horse I've ever known has given freely to me their friendship, time, energy, willingness and spirit ... I feel I owe them nothing less.

Gitty Up ~ *Dutch Henry*

Paddock Paradise and the Track System
For the Health of Your Horse

Howdy Friends,

Horses love to move about. After years of studying and observing wild horses in the Great Basin of the west, former farrier Jaime Jackson not only gained a deep understanding of the natural ways of the horse, but he also learned how horses move in the wild. He put his observations on horse movement, travels, health and habits into his book "Paddock Paradise." I highly recommend it. You can buy his book on his web site http://www.jaimejackson.com/ and Amazon—in it he clearly explains his observations and details how anyone, anywhere, can create a track system for their horses. You can also make a lot of friends on the Paddock Paradise Facebook page who have implemented this practice for their own horses.

One of the many things Jaime observed, noted and proved was that horses, left to their own choices in the wild, move along regular tracks. They have well established routes, or tracks, for grazing areas, watering, resting, foraging and even playing. They don't graze in lush grass, they nibble and browse while moving. It is these known facts that he incorporated into his idea of Paddock Paradise, and many folks have adopted. I believe it is the most natural and healthiest way to house and keep a horse.

The track system goes hand in hand with maintaining a barefoot horse's feet to be strong, beautiful, and healthy. Movement is a key ingredient to the barefoot paradigm, and nothing I have ever seen encourages movement as well as the track system. Lush grass and continuous grazing are as unnatural to a horse

as couch potato sitting and gorging is to humans
… but we lazy humans force it on our horses, then
wonder about a plethora of equine health issues from
insulin resistance to laminitis. Stalls, barns, pastures
and shoes are a human convenience, not a horse-first
philosophy.

Many times folks say "It looks too inconvenient or
expensive to set up." To that I say, in the long run, and
even the not-so-long run, it will be far less expensive
than vet bills, injuries and anguish—the person's
and the horse's—and missed riding and competing
dates. Yes the track system works for shod as well
as barefoot horses … and folks who know me know
I believe every horse should be barefoot. One very
wrong answer to the "too much grass" syndrome is
to confine their horses in stalls, use poorly designed
grazing muzzles, small paddocks or "sacrifice" lots.
Rubbish all. None of these things are either natural to
a horse, or healthy to their bodies or minds. Let the
horses roam at will, I say.

Paddock Paradise, or the track system, incorporates
every aspect of a horse's natural and instinctive urge
and desire to be on the move. Explained briefly, the
track system is a track 10 to 20 feet wide inside your
already existing big pasture (which may have too
much grass) with various footings such as dirt, pea
gravel and rocks. Also incorporated within the track
are wide places for play, sleeping and rolling, as well
as hay feeding stations and watering locations, and
run-ins, strategically placed to encourage and support
movement. Many folks add mud holes, streams and
bridges to help their horses overcome issues, or just
for fun and variety.

Your track can be any design that fits your land, plan
and budget. I once saw a terrific track on an acre and

a half rocky, grassy hillside that offered long winding trails instead of just a useless hang out spot.

Many folks, when they set up their first track, simply use step-in posts with electric fence, easy and very affordable, and if the horses escape the track, they're still within the original pasture. Of course the original grass pasture can be opened for limited grazing with far less risk of overeating and all the health problems associated with the high sugar content of most pasture and field grasses.

Another common objection to creating the track system is "We have all this grass and we can't afford to not use it." Some folks then bale it or even graze a few cows on it. Sometimes it takes years for the symptoms of sugar-related health issues to show up in horses, but don't be fooled, eventually symptoms are likely to occur—often not connected to the true cause of too much grass and not enough movement.

The Paddock Paradise and track system is the easiest, best choice for maintaining a healthy horse and healthy hooves.

For the health and happiness of horses everywhere, it is my hope many more people begin to see horse care from the horse's perspective.

Gitty Up ~ *Dutch Henry*

My Mare's Diet

◆────⟨✸⟩────◆

Howdy Friends,

Recently a few friends asked about my feeding protocol for Kessy. I'm a simple fellow, and as in everything I do I like to keep feeding simple too. Sure, years ago when I played in the competitive trail and endurance world, I bought into feeding all this, and lots of that, all kind of seeds, grain, beet pulp, supplements and on and on. But I soon realized what I reasoned to be the many problems with all that.

As I said last week during our Coffee Clutch ("Practices for a Healthy, Happy Horse"), "Horses are designed to be forage eaters." It is my belief that, just as with we humans, most health issues can be traced to diet and exercise. The epidemic of ulcers in horses is just one ready example. My personal rule for all things equine is "No shoes, no stalls, no grain, limited grass and seeing everything from the horse's point of view."

Kessy's nutritional protocol is very simple, and part of that protocol is housing. Exercise is key to good health and I include it in any diet discussion. Kessy enjoys a Paddock Paradise habitat in the trees, no grass, a run-in, no stall.

We use one-inch slow-feeder hay nets located at several locations in her paradise to encourage movement. We feed tested hay, and I weigh each bag. Kessy weighs 925 pounds; she gets a total of 20 pounds of hay per day in her nets plus one pound of soaked hay cubes twice per day.

I fill the bags morning and evening, exactly 5 pounds in each of two bags—the one-inch nets keep her happily busy for the day and night. I hang the bags so they just touch the ground so she is eating in the grazing potion. Note: in cold weather, I increase her hay to as much as 35 or pounds or more; horses need long-stem forage to fuel the furnace.

Mornings she also gets exactly one pound of soaked timothy cubes. In that I mix, 1 teaspoon sea salt, her enzymes and vitamins ... I have used Advanced Biological Concepts products for 15 years; they are totally organic and GMO-free, and I'm happy to recommend them and their support team. I feed their ABC-Plus Enzymes, their A and B mix vitamins and Rush Creek minerals. Minerals are free choice as well as Redmond salt. Water of course is always available and the tub kept spotless.

Evenings Kessy gets another pound of soaked timothy cubes with her enzymes and, because it is impossible to achieve optimum health without adequate micronutrients Kessy gets 1 scoop SOURCE® Micronutrients, a seaweed based supplement I highly recommend. Bedtime she gets a handful of fresh vegetables and a slice of apple.

I am very careful to make sure her hay is tested and "low sugar," less than 10% NSC. Kessy became insulin resistant a few years ago after a bout of Lyme disease.

That's it, simple. I see no need for costly and crazy supplements that can confuse the digestive system and even the immune system. Kessy looks great, hoofs are rock-crushing hard, coat as glossy as a new penny, eyes glistening, attitude sharp. She's a happy girl, and that makes me happy.

Gitty Up ~ *Dutch Henry*

Do You Know What's in Your Hay?

Howdy Friends,

Be sure to test your hay. In many cases, the sugar
and non-structured carbs are higher than we think.
Your county extension agent will happily test it for
you. Best horse hay will be no higher than 10%
non-structured carbs, or sugar. Kessy became insulin
resistant (IR) after her bout with Lyme disease and
I noticed the "fat patches" building even though I
was feeding Teff hay, which by all studies done at
universities suggested was a low sugar hay. Penn
State even suggested it for IR and obese horses.
Kessy continued to build fatty splotches and even
started a cresty neck, even though she gets no grain
and no grass. So I finally tested my hay (yes I knew I
should have sooner and have no excuse for not having
done it). To everyone's surprise it came back 15%
non-structured carbs and sugar, 17% protein! I did
then soak her hay for an hour or so before each meal,
which will remove about 20% of the sugar, but this
also removes vitamins and minerals as well.

It seems today we are seeing way too many IR horses.
Are there truly more, or are we just becoming more
aware of what to look for? That's a good question,
but whatever the answer, we need to focus on how we
might prevent and/or manage our horses.

Many forages were researched and developed for
cows. Most cool season grasses found in horse
pastures and hayfields are today high in sugar.
Recently, even the old standby orchard grass was
found often to be high in sugar. Timothy seems to
be medium in its sugar content, but is hard to find in
many areas. Alfalfa is not a good answer because it
tends to be higher in digestible energy, calories and

protein than grasses. More calories can create weight gain, and too much protein is not great for horses.

What can we do? Of course testing is very important to know your hay's sugar content. **Mowing hay early in the morning can help; sugar tends to be lower then if temperatures are above freezing**. Limit access to pasture, especially for overweight horses. **Laminitis does not usually occur "overnight"**; rather, it's the result of cumulative buildups. If you find you've purchased a good supply of hay, then test and you discover high sugar, as I did, you have the choice of soaking each flake for 20 or so minutes before feeding.

Horses are tough and will carry on even if things are not as they should be and we go merrily along not realizing we are setting them up for problems. And then we wonder when the problems are upon us, "How did this happen?"

For peace of mind, "Don't Guess, Test."

Gitty Up ~ *Dutch Henry*

Why Barefoot?

H owdy Folks,

I had a catchier title in mind, but by golly "Why Barefoot?" seems to ask the most important question. The answer is, of course, it's best for the horse. There you go. That's it. I could stop there and have my shortest blog-post ever, but you know me, so I'll go on a bit. First I need to thank my mentor, Diane Sept, for opening my mind to the health benefits and well being of allowing horses to go barefoot. The health benefits, you might ask? How can a hoof, unprotected by a steel or aluminum shoe, be healthy for a horse? I'll give a few thoughts as I've learned them over the years.

Nutrients and blood flow. By design the blood flow through the hoof—and leg, tendons and muscles for that matter—is aided by the natural expansion and contraction of the hoof as it contacts and raises off the ground. Contact causes expansion of the hoof, lifting allows contraction. Think of it as a syringe sucking up fresh blood loaded with oxygen and nutrients as you pull back the plunger, and then squirting out the stale blood loaded with toxins and depleted of oxygen as you depress the plunger, sending it back through the heart, lungs, kidneys and other organs to be refreshed, cleansed and oxygen enriched to begin the cycle all over again.

Nailing shoes on the hoof greatly inhibits the ability of the hoof to perform this all-necessary and vital function by preventing the hoof from expanding and contracting properly. That's why you see shod hooves that look flaky and full of tiny cracks, and frogs that are narrow, misshapen and weak. And soles that are hard, cracked and lifeless. These hooves are

STARVED for nutrients and loaded with toxins they have no way of shedding because the hoof cannot operate as designed. I suppose these poor starved, lifeless hooves are the reason for the huge industry out there of feed supplements for healthy hooves (which can hardly get there anyway if the hoof pump isn't working) and the products to paint and smear on the hoof to make the flakes and cracks go away, or hide them. Why not simply remove the shoes so the horse can heal its hooves without all those chemicals, and save you money, too?

Shape of the hoof. There is simply no way for a hoof to enjoy the healthy conformation it was designed to have with a shoe nailed, or glued to it. For one thing, when farriers prepare a hoof for a shoe, they file the bottom of the walls flat. Horses' hoof walls are not flat on the bottom by natural design; they have an arch, much like our own foot. The toe and heel of the hoof wall will touch the ground while the center of the hoof wall will be slightly raised, only touching the ground as the hoof is in motion. This natural action and flexing is prohibited by the restriction of the shoe, causing the foot to smack the ground more like a club than a graceful dancer's foot.

Shape of the hoof, continued. Typically, shod hooves have longer, or higher heels, and usually longer toes than is healthy for the horse. These incorrect and unhealthy conditions greatly change the angle of the pastern, ankle, leg and shoulder, causing discomfort and excessive wear and tear on many other joints and muscles throughout the body. Of course there's another entire industry out there ready to take your money and pollute your horse's bloodstream with supplements for stiff joints and achy muscles. Why not give nature a try first through healthy hooves?

Horses see with their feet. Yes, that's right. Horses have a wonderful way of seeing the ground through their hooves, which is why when you ride a barefoot horse, stumbling, missteps and over-reaching are rare things indeed. With shoes nailed to the feet and blood flow restricted, it's like tying a blindfold on their feet. They really just don't know where their own feet are, and are compensating with other senses not designed to focus so heavily on foot placement.

Shock absorption. The hoof is the primary means of shock absorption for the horse's entire body. Through natural flexion, expansion and contraction, the hoof absorbs and disperses the shock of the hoof striking the ground. The shoe not only prohibits that natural and vital function but it instantly sends the shock up through the body where it must be absorbed by joints, bones, muscles and tendons not designed as shock absorbers, causing excessive wear and tear, and pain ... There is, though, that helpful industry out there to sell you supplements and pain medicine for your horse, caused by that shock transference. And there's even "corrective shoeing" available for helping with those injuries. For me, "corrective shoeing" feels like an oxymoron.

Traction. A healthy hoof has a wide, long frog offering support to both shock absorption and traction. Healthy hooves will grip the ground and snow very effectively. And you won't have those snowballs forming as in a steel shoe. I submit even on paved roads, the natural, healthy hoof has wonderful traction, and in years past I too believed you needed shoes with borium or studs to travel safely on paved roads.

So, "Why Barefoot?" I still think the best answer to that question is "It's best for the horse." Please join us tomorrow for some helpful thoughts on how to make the transition from shod to barefoot.

Gitty Up ~ *Dutch Henry*

How Can I Transition to Barefoot?

Howdy Folks,

Yesterday I shared a few thoughts on the healthy reasons to go barefoot. Of course in one blog post, even a long one, not everything could be covered, but I hope I hit the most important reasons—nutrients and blood flow, shape of the hoof, horses see with their feet, shock absorption and traction.

As I said yesterday, I owe my understanding of the health benefits to the horse by going barefoot to my mentor, Diane Sept. And folks, she'll tell you, I was not an easy convert. But she's patient, kind and really very knowledgeable. I think back now of a few of the horses in my past and wonder if they may have fared better had she won that battle with me sooner. One magnificent horse in particular, my Diablo. A Spotted Saddle Horse who began his career long before I met him, in the show ring dealing with those horrible shoeing and other practices designed to "Make A Gaited Horse Gait." That's a topic for another day ... But Diablo was a tremendous horse who developed such bad arthritis in his front ankles that a month before his tenth birthday he was unable to even stand. I wonder often had I allowed him to go barefoot from the day we met, would he have had a longer life?

Is it easy to transition a horse from shoes to barefoot? I say YES! We have any number of safe, easy to put on, and suitable for anything you want to do with your horse, hoof boots. Hoof boots have made much progress, are available everywhere and not only hold up well but also will save you money compared to shoeing. Many endurance riders use boots on 100-mile and multi-day rides.

How do you go about the transition? I say jump right in, the water's lovely. Your horse will think so too. There are great resources and folks out there to help you. If you've not found a barefoot trimmer, search the web for "Certified Barefoot Trimmers." Aside from my mentor Diane, the main resource for me were the books of Jaime Jackson, whom I credit with really being the fellow who first shined the light on the benefits of going barefoot, and Pete Ramey. Pete has on his website much valuable information and a link to help you find a trimmer. Another wonderful resource is Joe Camp. Joe has on his website a link to help you find a trimmer and a list of 10 excellent questions to ask before hiring a trimmer.

First know it is natural to take some time. Depending on the horse, it could take 6 months, a year, or no time at all. Please don't let that stop you. From the moment you pull those shoes your horse will begin to enjoy the benefits of better health. And you could be going along smoothly right from the start, even as the hooves change. The first hoof to grow out takes about a year. The second regrowth will come in with a greater density. And of course during this time, use hoof boots as you need them. As I said earlier, there are a good number of quality hoof boots to choose from. The most important thing with the boots is to size them correctly, and every manufacturer I've seen has easy to follow directions for that. But you can, and should, be riding all along, and don't use the boots all the time. I've transitioned horses without the use of boots at all.

Trimming a barefoot hoof is different than a farrier just pulling shoes and letting a bare hoof hit the ground. Be sure to find a barefoot practitioner who understands this. *My personal belief is if the hoof care provider also does steel shoes, choose someone else, for anyone who can nail shoes to a live hoof does not understand the biomechanics of the foot or the horse.*

The first thing to do when pulling the shoes is to **file only the toe** back to where it should be—**from the top down**—do nothing on the bottom. Make a promise to never again trim the frog or scrape off sole ... **leave the bottom of the foot alone**. Then give her a few days or a week or so to move about, as she will be shaping her hoof as it should be—making the arch, lowering the heel and flexing the sole. Movement is KEY at this time, so be sure she has room to roam—standing on soft grass or in a bedded stall **will accomplish nothing**. Check out "The Paddock Paradise" track system from Jaime Jackson. Note— Some toes are so long you may not be able to file them back to the correct length the first time. Work on it over the coming weeks. The toe length guideline is that "one-third of the hoof should be in front of the frog apex (tip)."

When the shoes are first pulled and your horse seems to be "ouchy," what is happening is blood is flowing into the hoof and awakening nerves that had been shut down. Too many times folks mistake this for thinking their horse cannot go without shoes, so they put them back on. With shoes back, they appear to be sound again when really all that's happened is the nerves have been blood-starved again, so the foot has lost the ability to feel again. It's not sound, it's numb. Give it time, in a few days it'll work out.

Put your horse out in the yard or pasture. Make sure she has plenty of room to move about, pump that blood. That's very important! If you see her picking her way along a soft route at first, keep an eye on it, but that is perfectly natural. She knows what she's doing, and she's beginning to see with her feet again. There is a lot going on. **Allow it to happen.** Remember her feet are just beginning to wake up. It may not hurt as much as just feel strange to her. Put her hay at several different locations so she's encouraged to walk about. Put down pea gravel in areas she must walk over. Pea gravel is remarkable at massaging and helping hooves become rock-crushing tough and lively.

Don't be afraid to ride. **Riding is important to the transition.** Use boots at first if you must. But here I'd like to say as you go down the trail, **let her select the path she feels best about.** If she wants to go along the edge where there is grass or soft earth, let her. As time goes on and her feet become healthy, that'll change.

I hope I've encouraged you if you're thinking about giving your horse the health and freedom of going barefoot. I realize I did not give a grand outline. There isn't one. Just surround yourself, and your horse with supporters, not doubters, check out the websites I've listed, and others you will find, and listen to your horse ... Perhaps I could have listened to Diablo.

Gitty Up ~ *Dutch Henry*

Going Barefoot,
Sometimes a Touchy Subject
‹✦›

Howdy Friends,

One uncomfortable thing many folks who have decided to take their horses barefoot face is peer pressure. They've made the decision based on facts we now know to be true: "No shoe can be applied to a hoof without damage and health compromises." Read more in my blog, "Why Barefoot?" Sure, it can be a tough decision. Many folks labor with it for months, some years. Then they hear their horse and realize they must do the right thing.

The transition to barefoot, though, is just the beginning. The horse and their person must not only adjust to the new, healthier lifestyle, but often these horses are boarded in barns where many, if not most, have yet to see the light, and will insist going barefoot sets your horse up for failure and pain. To justify their own reluctance to change, or even honestly consider the health of their horse, they make excuses; it's too rocky here, my horse goes lame when it loses one shoe, how could it go barefoot, I tried it already and my horse could hardly walk, and on and on with the tired old reasons to justify nailing iron on hooves.

Sadly, in some cases, the peer pressure is so intense that folks just give up and don't make the transition to the barefoot paradigm. Some folks go on carrying the tug at their heart, deep inside knowing they should make the correct choice for their horse, but can't deal with the pressure at the barn. Others actually join those who "talked them out of barefoot," to try to placate that little voice inside that keeps telling them, "barefoot is healthier for your horse."

Peer pressure can be very difficult to deal with when a person is already nervous about making a change — even when that change is clearly for the better health of your horse. Haven't we all heard we should not allow negativity into our lives? Peer pressure is one of the most powerful forms of negativity. Folks who know going barefoot is best for their horse, but hesitate because they don't want to be an outsider in their barn, may simply need to find another barn and shed that negativity. It's for the horse, after all.

Another "touchy subject," referring to my title of this post. And please forgive my brashness with this one … but not all barefoot trimmers get it. My single biggest piece of advice here is, if your trimmer does barefoot as well as shoes, get another trimmer. They don't understand the workings of a horse's foot, legs and body, and are unable to see the true bare foot. They just see a foot without shoes. And that's not good enough.

On that note, I have a story. Recently I was invited to a barn to do some therapy exercises for two horses and instruct the owner on them. I don't know what percent of the horses there were barefoot, but the two I was to work on were. As I approached the first horse, while still a good 50 feet away, I could see the cause of the overall body pain of the handsome 4-year-old. His stance was one of managed discomfort, because it was all he knew. He was a sweet fellow with a kind look. I actually heard him say, "Help me." I turned to his owner and said, "Please forgive me for my bluntness, but before I even touch him, I can see where 100% of his soreness originates. His feet are horribly trimmed." The owner told me the "farrier" has been doing it for 30 years. I replied, "He's been doing it wrong that long too."

We did have a lovely session with the two horses, both of whom had the same badly managed hooves by the barn's 30-year veteran. I mixed in a few suggestions of what needed to be corrected, and a strong suggestion the owner switch trimmers, even recommended one. The owner informed me there is a lot of loyalty at the barn for this fellow and she was afraid to cause problems. The owner would "think about it." I was asked to continue to instruct the therapy exercises, which of course I'll do, but I left knowing those two sweet horses would continue to walk with pain from hooves caused by stretching lamina from incorrectly managed hooves, all the result of peer pressure.

I know this post is a bit edgier than I like to write, but I intend it in an honest, helpful way. As folks who know me understand, everything I write has its root in my motto, "It's for the Horses." If you are dealing with doubt, questions or peer pressure regarding anything about barefoot horsekeeping, I hope this little story helps strengthen your resolve.

Gitty Up ~ *Dutch Henry*

The Barefoot Paradigm

<big>H</big>owdy Folks,

On Monday our Coffee Clutch was "Going Barefoot—Sometimes a Touchy Subject," and it surely can be, for the horses, their people and friends. I'm a supporter of the barefoot paradigm, not any surprise to folks who know me. But what is the Barefoot Paradigm? I can only speak for myself, as I'm always ready to do. (That was supposed to make you smile.)

To me, the barefoot paradigm is about the whole horse. It's really a way of life. I believe it embraces the holistic approach to living with, loving and enjoying horses. Do as little as possible that might upset the natural lifestyle of the horse. Every horse caregiver has limitations; financial, geographic, time, conditions, housing and so forth. There are always decisions to be made—some easy, some challenging. If we make those decisions from the horse's perspective those decisions can often be made less challenging. Many times decisions made by horse caregivers are made for, and by, the human's perspective—and these can be in contradiction with the barefoot paradigm.

Much of what I consider the barefoot paradigm is really simply good horse sense. What are the most important things to keeping a horse happy, healthy and thriving? The barefoot paradigm is not only about yanking shoes, or never putting them on—it's about a lifestyle that promotes total health, as close to the natural state as possible for the caregiver to provide. We don't all have large, sparsely grassed acreage for them to romp free on. But we can say no to stalls, and yes to run-ins on as large a Paddock Paradise track system as possible. And we can make that track system resemble wide-open spaces by placing our water and slow-feeder hay nets" here and there to encourage movement. We can add obstacles or even allow trees and brush to add a little dimension to our horses' wanderings. Free and roaming movement is paramount to the health of a horse's hoof, and to the entire horse.

We can say no to grain, creating a healthy, all-forage diet. We can test our hay so we know what, if any, high quality supplements are needed. We can sprinkle fresh vegetables on the hay bags, for fun and nutrients. I'll not talk about vaccinations here, but it is something I consider in my barefoot paradigm. As are all unnatural chemicals, feeds, treatments and applications. Keep in mind, toxins travel to settle in the feet, so if we don't introduce them, or greatly limit them, they can't get lodged in our horse's hooves.

So you see, for me, the barefoot paradigm is about considering the horse's health, wellbeing and happiness first in our management practices. Housing that provides for uninhibited exercise, fresh air and engagement. Nutrition in line with what their bodies are designed to understand. And keeping as many toxins out of their systems as possible. It's just about that simple. Of course there is also hoof care to consider.

If a horse is being transitioned from shod to barefoot, the first thing to do is simply remove the shoes, and with a rasp take the toes back where they should be, and nothing else. Give the horse a few days or a week to begin to shape the hoof to a more natural state. Then select a qualified barefoot hoofcare specialist to maintain the hooves. Barefoot care should really be scheduled every 3 - 4 weeks, but that may vary some depending on riding, terrain etc.

Hoofcare and maintenance in the barefoot paradigm is really surprisingly simple. Today you can find a wealth of information out there. l suggest Yvonne Welz's quarterly magazine, "The Horse's Hoof." I highly recommend subscribing to it. You'll find her web site on the resources page.

I write for, and surely recommend Natural Horse Magazine, as well. You'll find their web site on the resources page.

There you have it, my thoughts on the barefoot paradigm. Really, there's nothing to it. It's just a little different in the way we do some things as humans. But it can make a world of difference for the horses.

Gitty Up ~ *Dutch Henry*

For a Beautiful Barefoot Trim
Keep It Simple

—————◇—————

Howdy Friends,

Kessy's never had shoes in her 12 years. She came to me at seven. I touch up her feet every three weeks as I believe for healthy bare feet, most horses are best served with a 3- to 4-week schedule. An 8- to 10-week schedule is too long and can encourage flares, stretching of the laminae or white line disease.

I maintain Kessy's feet with a sharp rasp, do all the shaping from the top down, holding the rasp on a good angle (see photo) so we get a good bevel, or mustang roll, as Jaime Jackson calls it. Every thought in this story comes from what I've read, seen and experienced, and by that formed my own opinion. I share my thoughts with the hope some folks may benefit, but they are my thoughts, so feel free to question them. Note—this is a maintenance trim, if your horse has problems you should find a professional, but this simple guide can fix many problems.

While rasping from the top down, I only work on the area to bevel, and angle my rasp to get that nice bevel, about ¾ of an inch. I never rasp down over the entire hoof to "clean it up," as we see so often, as that removes precious live material important for sealing, growth and hoof health. I look at the sole before I start, clean it with a stiff brush, not a hoof knife. Another opinion I have is we clean our horses' hoofs far too often and thereby strip away important live tissues put there to guard against disease and infection. If the horse has room to roam with pea gravel or other hard surface, she will keep her feet

clean and healthy. I think I clean Kessy's feet twice a
year with a hoof pick, some years not that often. From
the bottom, I judge toe length, heel growth, balance,
heel bars, etc. I only trim the bars if they are long
enough to fold over, which is rare for me indeed.

The view from the bottom tells me most of what I
need to do. Then I set her foot down have a look at
balance, position and angle, and start rasping at the
toe. The toe is my guide, because if the horse is well
maintained, she will always tell you where the toe
should be by wear. (Ideally, no more than one third of
the hoof should be in front of the apex of the frog.)

Here you can see Kessy's left hind foot measures 4½ inches front to back. The apex of her big beautiful frog is at about 1½ inches, exactly one third of the length of the weight-bearing part of sole. You can also see how great the frog looks and the beautiful sole. She walks on her sole as designed, not on the hoof wall. There is no black line of separation between sole and hoof wall, there should never be. If your horse has that, the toes are most likely too long, causing poor foot placement and challenged hoof health—as simple as that. All of her feet look this great.

If the bottom inspection tells me the heels are slightly out of balance, or a flare wants to start (which is never in my case, but wanted to mention because often a flare will tip its hand on the bottom before even showing an angle change on the hoof wall). I angle my rasp even more sharply in those areas to thin the wall more there so she can wear away the wall that needs to go and shape her hoof naturally in a way best for her.

And that's about all I do. I do not trim the frog, or pare or scrape the sole. That again removes precious live, or dead, tissue that is there for a reason. It will wear away naturally when she moves about. I rasp the wall even with the sole so she walks as designed on her sole, not her hoof wall. That helps prevent that ugly black line around sole and hoof wall, which can allow disease and infection into the laminae, and of course allows the suspensory tissues within the foot to remain tough, vigorous and strong and not weakened by excessive stretching, and builds rock-tough soles. One last thought about rasping only from the top down and following the hoof, in that way I can maintain the natural arch in Kessy foot, yes the hoof wall does and must have an arch, something that cannot be maintained by rasping flat across the bottom of the foot.

Of course trimming is only one part of a healthy barefoot horse. Housing, exercise, diet and health care all are equally important. I've thought about writing this story for a while now because there seems to be a lot of folks making barefoot trimming too complicated. It's not. Keep it simple, and leave the bottom and soles alone.

Gitty Up ~ *Dutch Henry*

KESSY'S BEAUTIFUL FEET

My Thoughts on Blanketing Horses

Howdy Folks,

One of our Coffee Clutch friends asked me to share my thoughts on blanketing horses. Like many things we do for, with and to our horses, there are mountains of opinions about whether "to blanket or not to blanket." I'm strongly in the "no blanket" camp. I reckon few of our Coffee Clutch friends are surprised by that, given that my keeping it truly natural practices and beliefs are not much of a secret.

But what is wrong with blanketing? I think a lot.

Now before we get all excited with the exceptions as to "Yes, but you must blanket when — insert any favorite exception here — because ..." I understand and agree, sometimes blankets are necessary and important. I also believe wool coolers are very important after a cold winter ride and a nice, thick winter coat is soaked and matted with sweat. Wool coolers wick away sweat and help a horse cool down nicely. Kessy wore one Sunday after we had a fun romp. Took only about 20 minutes for her to dry, I removed the cooler, brushed her all nice and fluffy, and she went about her way wearing only her smile and her own winter coat.

Horses have multiple layers of hair to deal with all sorts of weather, rain, cold and snow. Each layer has its own job and function. Even with snow lying on their backs, those layers do their job admirably — UNLESS their hair is wadded down under a blanket. Did you know a horse with a wet blanket, or even a waterproof blanket with snow on top of it, is actually colder than a horse without a blanket at all? I've personally demonstrated this by sliding my hand under a wet, but not soaked, blanket and the owner was surprised to feel the cold back.

Temperatures under a blanket with air temperatures about 40 or 50 can be over 70, sometimes close to 90. If you blanket, check it yourself.

Wearing a blanket prevents normal winter coat growth—they can't grow those very important layers.

Horses with a natural healthy coat can readily, and healthily, regulate their own body temperature, changing with the temperatures of the day. Hairs stand up and lay down as needed. How can we think we can manage that by taking off and on the blankets? We can't. Blankets also disrupt their internal regulator and while the body may be toasty, the exposed legs and neck may not be getting the warm blood needed to keep those exposed areas warm and safe.

Horses have several ways to "warm up" on cold days. They can walk around, this goes hand in hand with natural and healthy housing, they need room to roam, or they can shiver. Sometimes a horse will choose to stand still and shiver. This is natural, and not necessarily a sign of a cold horse. She just might be sleepy. But you should check if your horse is shivering. What they do need is a way to get out of the precipitation and wind, just a nice run-in where they can come and go as they please.

So, my thoughts on blanketing horses? I think most folks do it for their own thoughts of comfort, not the horses. Tack shops love that, by the way.

Yes of course, sick, clipped and aged horses may need blankets, but to sum it up, I'm against routine blanketing. I truly believe it's unhealthy for the horse.

Gitty Up ~ *Dutch Henry*

My Thoughts on Having One Horse

Howdy Folks,

Last week I was asked if I would share my thoughts on having just a single horse. My reason for wanting to keep only one horse is both health and financially driven. If I could I would have 3 to 5 as we used to. Coffee Clutch followers and Facebook friends know that I do have only one horse, my mare Kessy. You may not know that before Kessy, I had other single horses, my competitive trail/endurance horse River and the fabulous rescue horse Honey. All did fine being the only horse here.

Allow me to describe "here," because I do believe their home environment plays a big part. A barn that allows Kessy to come and go as she pleases, a bit over an acre to roam in among trees in a Paddock Paradise-style play area. No grass to speak of, but free choice hay in slow-feed hay bags 24/7. No grain, but some fruit and fresh vegetables. She also has her free roaming chickens, four cats and our dog, Saturday. Her barn is 30 feet from the house and her playground is our backyard, so she can and will come right up to the back door. Sometimes she'll nicker to get my attention.

Kessy has been an "only horse" for nearly 5 years; she moved in with us in May 2010. Kessy had never been off the farm where she was born, and she was 7. They had lots of horses, but Kessy even there was in her own field and woods. I believe she made the adjustment to being an only horse at our house right away. So did River and Honey, but as I said, I suppose their "home" here had something to do with it, the freestyle roaming and pets and chickens, and our back porch. And don't forget I start each day with our Coffee Clutch. And sometimes I write in the barn, but only when it's warm. Now everyone who would like to keep only one horse may not be able to do everything we do here, but I share our set up as "food for thought." Perhaps it might help you to make your own plans.

Also I do a fair amount with Kessy, including the release and relax exercises, riding two to three days per week, grooming almost daily and other little things. But there are plenty of days that all I do is feed her, too.

I've been told because of the herd thing, horses need other horses to be happy, they are herd animals, they say. Plenty of folks with one horse have ponies or minis as pasture buddies, or other companion horses. I think that is wonderful, if you want it. I was told a few years back, after River left and I was looking to adopt a horse, I could not adopt with only one horse, I needed at least a companion horse. I did not adopt there and often wondered: did that horse I wanted to give a home to find one? I hope so.

I know this is a touchy subject with strong opinions on both sides, but it's my opinion a horse can and will thrive and enjoy life if they are the only horse. Just as is the case with any horse, be it your only horse or part of a herd, how we care for, play with and learn from them are the most important things to that horse.

One final note: Kessy is just fine when we go riding with others, too. No excitement, no separation anxiety, no crowding on the trail. She is confident in herself, trusts me and enjoys herself. I think everyone needs to make this decision for themselves, but I think a single horse well cared for is perfectly wonderful. I also have several friends who have only one horse, and they are doing splendidly. I do think diet, exercise and no confinement to a stall are very important, but then I think that is very important for all horses.

Gitty Up ~ *Dutch Henry*

Balance Starts in a Horse's Mouth

———————⟨✦⟩———————

Howdy Folks,

We all know the importance of taking care of our horses' teeth and are sure to have our veterinarian or equine dentist visit annually. This weekend at the Equine Wellness Symposium, one of the presenters was Jamie Colder, and some of the things he discussed in his presentation are too important not to share.

We talk about balance in our horse's body and feet, and Jamie explained that balance cannot be achieved if there are issues in the teeth. Jamie discussed so much important information, much more than we can fit into a blog post, but I learned a few tips on Saturday that I just had to share here.

A horse has a very long jaw, and things out of order there get magnified by the movement of that long jaw. A horse is designed to chew by moving their mouth side to side and if they have misaligned teeth, or a hook (a tall tooth in the rear) they will "lift" their mouth open to avoid it when they chew. This causes muscles in the head and neck to strengthen to accommodate this abnormal motion. This also causes tightness in the neck and shoulder, making it difficult for the horse to turn into it. This little long tooth begins to set up a cascade of compensation that travels through the horse. Can even cause the feet to become out of balance. Jamie practices "Whole Horse Dentistry."

Jamie gave us lots of great tips on how we might see little signs that send signals we should address. One, of course, is if your horse has a tighter side than the other, your horse may have difficulty turning one way.

And yes, there are many reasons for this, but one just could be in the mouth. Or start there. He gave us a neat way to look for that "hook" tooth issue.

Lift your horse's forelock and study the top of her forehead. I certainly do not remember the names of the muscles up there, but study the forehead just below the base of her forelock, the big flat area, and look for muscling there. There really should be none—her forehead should be flat. If you see muscles, your horse is "lifting" her mouth to chew to avoid the long tooth, or "hook," then if you look closely you will see one side has more muscle than the other. That's the side of the hook tooth. These muscles only develop when the horse must lift to chew.

On Sunday I was doing a private session at the Symposium of "Therapy For Therapy Horses" exercises and as I went along and was relieving tightness I got to the "Cheek Wiggle" exercise. That's when you lightly rest one hand on the nose bridge, and with your fingertips of your other hand, gently hold the bottom of the cheek bone and very gently wiggle it. This releases the cheek, neck and poll. When I attempted the wiggle, I noticed the mare's jaw was ridged and locked. This exercise will release, and it did, but now armed with the new information I'd just learned from Jamie, I knew I must look further.

We lifted the mare's forelock and took a close look at her forehead. Sure enough, she had the telltale muscles just below the base of her forelock, and on the left side, the side of the "locked" cheekbone, was a larger muscle than on the right! Discovering that allows the horse owner to fix something that may have gone unnoticed. You can easily check your own horse just by studying her forehead and looking for those muscles.

But let me share one other quick test you can do to check for balance. Look at your horse's incisor teeth. Study the teeth with your horse's mouth closed, and look at the very center two teeth. Look at the space between them. The top and bottom space between the center incisors should line up perfectly. If they do not, something is off and you need your dentist. When we looked at the mare's incisors, we saw her spaces indeed did not line up, indicating even with her mouth closed her jaw was cocked to accommodate the hook tooth in the rear. And remember a horse's jaw is long. Think of the pressure and negative energy being sent through the body.

And yes, as soon as I got home Sunday night I did both these tests on Kessy, and am happy to report all is well.

I hope you will have a look at your horse's forehead and incisors. It's easy to do, and your horse will thank you!

Gitty Up ~ *Dutch Henry*

Natural Balance Dentistry

—————⟨✹⟩—————

Howdy Friends,

This chapter is excerpted from my story "What's the Point?" that I wrote for my Holistic Hall of Fame column in Natural Horse Magazine. There is so much important information here, I needed to include it in this book. Equine dental care is really just beginning to understand much more about equine oral health.

What's the Point?

"It's not about filing points, or just making horses eat," Spencer LaFlure, N.B.D., D.D.S., explained. "It's about the whole horse! Think of every tooth as a USB port sending information to all points throughout the horse. That is the very basis of our Natural Balance Dentistry."

Spencer went on to explain that indeed a horse's tooth is a calcium- and enamel-covered nerve, not simply a chewing device. "All balance in the horse begins in the mouth. If the mouth is out of balance, so is the horse," Spencer says. "Those nerves, and alignment of teeth and mouth positively or negatively, affect the balance, movement and of course the overall health of the horse."

While attending equine dentistry school, he continually noticed that horses' jaws seemed to be out of balance even after traditional dentistry was complete. "Hundreds of skulls were available to me there, and I studied them. Those skulls taught me many things, chief among them, the power tools not only took away too much, too fast, but we were working on the wrong end of the mouth first!" Spencer explained that realization was crystal clear to him, and it drove him to find a solution.

Tinkering with the skulls and putting into practice his ideas, he soon realized and understood what must change. The jaws must align to center the Temporomandibular Joint (TMJ). The TMJ is the canal through which the trigeminal nerve runs. "This nerve houses many other nerves that govern movements of the body, such as where the legs are positioned, how they move, how they feel, stride, balance and many other things we haven't even researched yet," Spencer explained. The only way to correctly align the jaws is from the front first. The incisors must be aligned first for the back of the mouth, the molars, to align and function properly. This proper alignment, he discovered, will not allow the creation of sharp edges, hooks and ramps. "If the mouth is properly aligned, the teeth will take care of themselves," Spencer explained.

Certain what he'd discovered was the answer to not only correct equine dentistry but also whole health issues with horses, he knew he must do whatever he could to help horses. "The problem with the way we've been practicing equine dentistry for hundreds of years is we're treating the symptom, not the cause. The sharp edges, ramps and hooks are all signs the jaw is out of alignment, not the root cause of the problem." Spencer explained. "And the problem with continually removing hooks and points is you reverse the natural plane of the molars, which puts pressure on the TMJ joint, which affects the whole horse negatively."

After five years of research and hundreds of case studies, he founded "Advanced Whole Horse Dentistry, Learning Center" to teach "Natural Balance Dentistry." He created new instruments for practitioners to work with—smaller, gentler instruments. "The adjustments needed to align the incisors is small, and I discovered we needed finer, non-power equipment."

Natural Balance Dentistry is not so much about eating, although they will eat better, as it is about posture, stride length, body mass (topline) and movement. Centering the trigeminal nerve is the basis for Natural Balance Dentistry. "The head and mouth is the very origin of balance for the horse. When the TMJ is out of alignment, so is everything else, and not only does performance suffer, but the pressure on the trigeminal nerve affects all aspects of comfort and health, even causing muscle atrophy," Spencer said.

Today there are graduates of Advanced Whole Horse Dentistry all across the country, indeed worldwide, helping horses retain their natural healthy balance. These practitioners work gently with the need of little or no sedation, with the horse's head in a natural position. "Our handheld instruments are configured to fit comfortably into the horses' mouth and short enough to get up close to keep track of every stroke and how much tooth is filed. The blades we use are 1" to 1½" long instead of 3" long for precision on every tooth," Spencer explained.

"The bottom line is that it is all about the total balance and health of your horse. What you should be looking for in dentistry is NOT an equine dentist but rather a Neuromuscular Natural Balance Dentist from Advanced Whole Horse Learning Center," Spencer said. "We have proven it with hundreds of horses and their owners who truly know their horses."

Natural Balance Dentistry may be new, but it's based on fact, and results, and like the barefoot movement is gaining momentum, because it works for the horse. Horses all over thank you Spencer for redefining the norm.

Gitty Up ~ *Dutch Henry*

Note: To learn more, and find a certified Natural Balance Dentist, please go to their website listed on the resource page.

A Pain in Your Horse's Back?

Howdy Folks,

I so often have folks email me with questions about their horses' backs. Many questions are concerning "dropped" backs and sagging toplines. Working with my mentor, Diane Sept, it was not uncommon to hear her say, "There's no reason a horse can't have a straight, firm topline into their 30s." Of course, as always, there may be exceptions, but for most of our horses, that's true.

What causes a horse to lose its firm, straight topline? A lot of things, mostly all in our control. Everything from saddle fit to teeth and mouth care, hoof care, to how we sit in the saddle, to how we lead our horse. And other things too—injuries, conformation and even nutrition.

Working with Diane, I learned much about the biomechanics of horses and the tremendous help we can give as caregivers to keep our horses moving freely in a posture and body carriage that maintains a correct, comfortable and healthy topline.

For me, I think the single biggest thing we can do is to be sure our horse is "off the forehand" and has an engaged hind end. There is a very simple way to accomplish this by the two of you mastering the "The Rock Back" exercise. Have a look, master it together and you'll see remarkable changes in health, politeness, body carriage and responsiveness.

Off the forehand (Rock Back exercise) is first, because it ties into everything else we do. And we can learn to lead, and ride, our horse off the forehand, and be sure to lead from both sides— this is so important for overall health and posture of your horse. And don't always walk in a straight line. Mix in long, soft, sweeping zigzags as you go along. Engage that hind end!

Next, let's mix in a few easy to learn exercises to do regularly, and certainly before we mount up. I have several exercises detailed with photos in **"Restarting, Conditioning and Great Exercises For Your Horse Pt 1, 2, 3, 4"** and noted those I always do pre-ride. These selected exercises done in a regular routine that fits your schedule will make a tremendous difference in the health of your horse.

Taking care of your horse's topline can be easy, fun and oh-so-good for her.

Gitty Up ~ *Dutch Henry*

NOTE – To see photos of these exercises, please go to the **"Restarting, Conditioning and Great Exercises For Your Horse Pt 1, 2, 3, 4"** section, where you'll find these and other exercises described with photos.

My Thoughts on Horse Vaccination

Howdy Friends,

Often I've been asked about my thoughts on horse vaccinations. Thoughts on vaccinations, as do many homeopathic, holistic and natural practices, such as all-forage diets, no stalls, no shoes, etc., often cause quite vigorous debates. I've resisted writing about vaccinations because it is so scary to so many horse lovers, owners and caregivers, I simply did not want to get into the debate. My own opinion though is we way, way over-vaccinate—to the health detriment of our horses (dogs, cats and children too).

Recently I had the thrill, honor and privilege of interviewing Dr. Will Falconer, one of this country's most respected homeopathic veterinarians, for a story in Natural Horse Magazine. Like most homeopathic veterinarians, his career began as doctor of veterinarian medicine. He is one of many homeopathic veterinarians or holistic practitioners I've interviewed over the years, and I've noticed a common thread of ideas, thoughts and concerns running through the minds of all these educated and experienced folks. In one way or another, they all found they wanted to do better. They wanted to find ways to truly help their patients live healthier, more thriving lives. Another common thread running through all their comments during our interviews was their concerns about vaccinations. My interview with Dr. Falconer finally prompted me to pen my thoughts on vaccinations.

I'll start with a quote from Dr. Falconer: "People simply do not relate or understand the harm that over vaccination does to the system. If there were one thing I could wave a magic wand and fix, it would be the attitude toward vaccinations." Dr. Falconer explained that repeated vaccinations impair and confuse the immune system.

"Most vaccinations for horses are for viruses, and veterinary immunologists have proven scientifically that, once vaccinated for a virus, resulting immunity lasts a very long time, perhaps a lifetime." Dr. Falconer explained that repeated vaccinations not only confuse the immune system but often cause it to turn on itself and even attack healthy red blood cells. "The horse is the most over-vaccinated animal, even more than dogs and cats, and repeated vaccinations do more damage than any other management practice. Repeated vaccination causes a plethora of ill effects that people fail to connect to the vaccine, including allergies, skin conditions, thrush and even changes in temperament. These are long-lasting effects that take their toll. If people would just have one awakening in their journey to have a vital, thriving animal, I wish it could be that they would understand, we now know, all vaccinations for viruses last a very long time, and repeated vaccinations to an already immune horse adds nothing, but it does compound the ill effects. In the late 1970s, vaccine researcher Dr. Ronald Schultz discovered that rabies and the core vaccines last for the life of the animal in nearly all cases."

I chose to use Dr. Falconer's quotes because he succinctly put some of the concerns that I've heard many times from others. So many ailments in our horses can be linked to repeated vaccinations, as Dr. Falconer said above, and even more than listed here. However, many veterinarians advise only to "Watch for symptoms for a few days," or words to that effect. While the truth is underlying chronic health issues that cause moderate to severe pain, lethargy, disinterest or even poor temperament are chronic health issues related to vaccines that can show up weeks or months later, and last a lifetime.

Worry about thrush, white line and founder? We all know that toxins in the horse migrate to the foot. There are toxins in vaccines that never really leave the body—toxins put into vaccines purposely to "stimulate the immune response." If it were not so horrendous that phrase would be silly, reminds me of the equally silly oxymoron, "corrective shoeing."

Another problem with vaccinations is the way they short-circuit the immune system. The immune system comes about 75% from the gut. Healthy digestive system = healthy immune system. But it is also supported by defenses throughout the body. The first line of defense is the nose, the throat and even tears. Each of these begins to attack the invader and signal the immune system to defend, attack and repel. Each of these areas of defense helps to educate and bolster the immune system. When we inject vaccinations directly into the body we skip all the front-line defenses, thus robbing the body of that innate knowledge and power. Another thing Dr. Falconer and others I've interviewed said was how we are seeing so many horses coming up with wide varieties of allergies. Immunologists have linked this to confused immune systems.

"A practice that was started many years ago and that lacks scientific validity or verification is annual revaccination. Almost without exception there is no immunologic requirement for annual revaccination. Immunity to viruses persists for years or for the life of the animal...... Furthermore, revaccination with most viral vaccines fails to stimulate an anamnestic (secondary) response.... The practice of annual vaccination, in our opinion, should be considered of questionable efficacy…" Excerpt from Current Veterinary Therapy, Volume XI, published in 1992 (a very well-respected, peer-reviewed textbook that is updated every four years). The authors are veterinary immunologists Dr. Ronald Schultz (University of Wisconsin) and Dr. Tom Phillips (Scripps Research Institute).

Immunology has recognized for a great many years that viruses provide a long-lived immunity. This is why your physician is not sending you postcards to repeat your small pox or polio vaccinations annually.

So why do so many veterinarians prescribe and recommend repeated vaccinations? That is a question only they can answer. Money? Profit? They truly believe it is best for their clients? The interesting thing is how many of them are beginning to question it. The whole vaccine issue is so difficult to get a handle on. Veterinarians are not taught much about immunology, just as they are not taught much about nutrition.

Many horse owners struggle with peer pressure inflicting fear, self doubt. Or you need to vaccinate to show, but do you really? Many folks believe they need vaccination certificates to travel, but I believe I'm accurate in saying no states require certificates of vaccination, only the Coggins test, and perhaps a veterinarian's health certificate. Some boarding barns require vaccinations—can this be negotiated? I would move my horse.

These are just my thoughts, I'm sharing them in the hopes you might think about it, and do some research of your own. There is plenty of information out there today. I believe in the "once is enough treatment for vaccinations." It is far better to learn how to help your horse build the strongest possible immune system that can defend against invaders, viruses included. Tetanus is the only vaccination that needs to be repeated every 7 years.

For me and my mare Kessy, she'll never have another vaccination, or shoe. Oh, and she has not been chemically wormed in four years either, just did a fecal count, no worms.

Gitty Up ~ *Dutch Henry*

SECTION VI

Horsemanship

In this section, I've included a fairly wide range of stories. Here are the stories I think you'll find helpful in areas from manners to politeness, partnering, saddle fit and more. A few stories deal with gaited horses, and these stories have thoughts in them that apply to all horses and their people.

Clarity — In Writing and Horses

Howdy Friends,

Ever since I started writing, I've been struck by how many things important in writing are also important in living with our horses. I've written about a few of them already; today we'll think about clarity.

I remember being told when my novel We'll Have The Summer was in the editing process at the publisher that they came across a scene that failed to totally embrace and engage the editor because it felt as if not all the information was there. I even remember the scene today. I remember I was horrified, since it was a very important scene and the story needed the reader to be crystal clear, completely consumed by Sam's worry, fear and reflection. What had I missed?

I read the scene and the pages leading up to it over and over, and to me everything was in place. It took me exactly where I wanted the story, the cadence and the tension to take the reader. So I called the editor and insisted they must be missing something, since it was very clear to me.

The editor was an understanding woman, and with kindness in her voice she explained. "That's often the case, as writers you can see the scene you want to write, you have all the information in your mind working for you. Your readers don't have those little tidbits, so the writer must be sure to convey them in their writing, so the reader has enough information to see clearly the story you are telling. But not too much information as to make it boring."

She then asked me one question that shined the light on my omission, and as I recall the fix proved to be a very simple few words. Those words I'll never forget were, "But not today."

There you have it, as writers we know the story. We know all the details, our job is to make sure we give those sparkling details to our readers, not in a boring "information dump" but in lively, engaging words and thoughts that sweep the reader along in the essence of the moment, the scene. We want them to have all the information so they can travel with us.

Every bit of this thought on "clarity" is equally important when we are working and playing with our horses. It is our responsibility to be sure we are crystal clear in our information, desires, requests — without giving a boring "information dump." We need to sweep them along in our scene. We know the complete story, our job is to convey that information in a kind, understanding way that will embrace them and carry our horses into our scene. Step back in our minds and ask ourselves, "How does my horse see this scene? I'm not being boring, am I? Are there enough sparkling details to tell her the whole story? "Be sure to write the scene so your horse can see the whole picture. For the pleasure of it."

Gitty Up ~ *Dutch Henry*

A Few Polite Touches For A Pushy Horse

Howdy Friends,

We've all seen horses crowd, drag or push their person when being led. I chuckle sometimes when I see folks follow the pace set by their horse as they are dragged along. I frown when I see them yank on the lead and yell at their horse. I feel sorry for them when they get stepped on, because neither of them knows where they are supposed to be, or their job. It simply does not need to be this way.

We are responsible for setting boundaries. Not by discipline or heavy handedness, but by simple politeness, consistency and thoughtfulness. Horses do not violate boundaries because they want to be bad, unruly or "pushy." They violate boundaries because their caregiver never set them, politely.

If you think about it, pushy horses follow exactly the boundaries set by their person. If each time a horse is haltered and led it drags their person, dances, steps on their feet and pushes them through the gate, well when the halter goes on and they set out, the horse has to think, "Okay time to drag, push, dance and I gotta be sure to try for her feet." It's never the horse's fault—they are well within the boundaries set by their person.

I once asked a friend, "Do you know why your horse holds her head so high when you try to halter her?" She replied, "No, tell me, I hate this." I said, "That's how high you can reach." Think about it seriously, any horse can lift their head higher than we can reach. If they can learn to hold their head at our highest limit, as they've been taught, does it not make sense they can also learn to hold their head waist high for halter and bridle? Sure it does. Our horses happily learn everything we teach them. They also learn from us to be rude and pushy, just like us.

Every horse will appreciate a partner who knows the correct way to put on a halter or bridle. The first step is to teach the horse to lower her head to a comfortable level for their partner, and the Poll Wiggle helps with this. Then the person needs to learn to UNBUCKLE the halter – NOT DRAG IT OVER THE EARS, and close it BEHIND THE EARS. Lowering her head is comfortable for the person, and very comfortable for the horse. Unbuckling the halter is not only correct, it is polite.

Now let's talk about the pushy horse on a lead line. Easy to fix, politely, in one lesson. I like to work on the off side whenever I'm fixing anything, or introducing something new. It heightens a horse's attention. Remember, we can never control any horse by the halter and lead rope. Ever. So forget about that. The halter is simply a gentle guide. I don't like the word control, anyway, so let's talk about guiding the horse, into their space, into our pace, and into softness and politeness.

For this exercise, which will become an all-the-time exercise for a really long time, you'll need a light dressage wand, or the new popular light bamboo wand. Not a crop, which is too short and stiff, or a longe whip, which is too long.

Stand on the off side, between her ears and shoulder; hold the lead rope in your left hand, your hand just about a foot or less from the halter. Hold the wand in your right hand, across your middle to a few inches in front of your horse's chest. It is important to **stand square, shoulders and eyes looking where you are going, not at the horse.** It is sometimes helpful to practice this stance, position and walk alone with the rope and wand, just to master the feel of it before trying it with a horse.

Ask your horse to "walk on" and start walking, holding the wand a few inches in front of her chest.

Eyes straight ahead. You may need to ever so slightly tap her chest, not hit it, until she figures it out. In time usually not much time at all, you'll need only to hold wand the in front of her chest and never touch her. The pushy, rude horse will never again be seen. As long as you clearly, gently and respectfully set the boundaries.

Notice how Kessy is completely concentrating on me, and she is off her forehand carrying herself in correct posture. This takes a little time but pays big dividends to person and horse. I am purposely on her right side, not only so you can see her beautiful mane but to demonstrate another technique I always use. Whenever I'm working with a horse the first time, I always do so on the right. Horses are so used to most things happening on their left that when things are introduced on the right, they focus.

One last thing: most horses become pushy because they are heavy on their forehand. Leading this way, every time, all the time, helps fix that. I suggest you also master the "Rock Back" and add it to your daily routine. To briefly recap this exercise, stand beside your ground-tied horse, facing her, and very gently touch her chest and ask her to "rock back." Not to take a step back but to simply shift her weight to her hind end, where it belongs. If she steps back, she'll stay on her forehand. Be soft, and look for only a tiny movement at first. After a few days she'll get it and you'll wonder where this polite, light footed, soft and confident horse came from.

So there you go—an easy way to help your horse understand boundaries, and correct body carriage, politely. Kessy and I hope you have fun with it. Remember politeness and consistency work like magic.

Gitty Up ~ *Dutch Henry*

Your Horse CAN Stand Still

◆———〈✦〉———◆

Howdy Friends,

Traveling to do clinics at therapeutic riding centers and rescues, it is pretty common to see horses who have a hard time standing still and comfortable. It's also pretty common to notice that after a few "release and relax" exercises, most of the horses have begun to stand quietly, and to hear folks comment, "Wow, he never stands this way for me."

When I'm demonstrating "Therapy For Therapy Horses," I think it's important to do the exercises with the horse not tied. They need to be able to move freely, which they can't really do while tied. Of course we're in a ring, corral or arena during the clinics, so they really can't run away, but with other horses in the ring with them and other people too, many horses step around, hold their heads high and worry. Showing the horses they can stand still during the clinics does work, but if you work on it at home, alone, devoted to just your horse, it works much better. So how about a few little exercises and tips to help with that? And friends, this will transfer into the saddle.

Horses can stand much more quietly if they are comfortable. One thing you can do to help is always ask your horse to "Rock Back" off the forehand. Just gently touch her chest and encourage her to rock back—i.e., shift her weight back without taking a step back. Another is to do the "Mane Wiggle." Firmly grasp her mane and wiggle, wiggle, wiggle, starting gently and increasing until you see her entire neck jiggling. She'll lower her head and relax.

Teaching your horse to stand "Ground Tied" is not hard to do and is very beneficial and relaxing for the horse. Start in an enclosed area by walking with your horse. I like to start on the off (right) side for this because horses are most often led on the left. Walk slow and easy a few moments, doing large sweeping figure eights. Begin mixing in a few stops, including the rock back (not a step back). Be sure to turn toward her when you ask for the "Whoa," and say it. Be sure she is standing comfortably when she stops. Wait each time for her to process the stop, stand still, and wait. Then say, "Stand." It's just the word I like to use. When you walk on, turn forward and say "Walk on," then start off gently.

When she's mastered a smooth, soft whoa and stand, add the next move. While facing her let go of your lead rope, making sure she sees you drop it, and say "Stand" again. I also like to hold my hand up in a stop fashion, and make solid eye contact in this learning phase. Now take one step back, continue to face her and wait about half a minute while you stand relaxed and soft. This is NOT a test to see if she moves. Rather it is a teaching, learning moment. Hopefully she will not move and you can step to her, pick up the lead, tell her what a good girl she is, like you mean it. Then turn, ask her to, "Walk On," and go back to the walking and gentle comfortable stops. Remember to hold your hand close to the halter as you walk, you want crystal clear connection. Do this several times, each time keeping the "Stand" time about the same short time, building confidence and consistency.

A BIG key to remember is, **should she move, even one foot, put her back EXACTLY where she was**. You are helping her to understand, "Stand means right here" not "It sort of means about here." **Consistency builds confidence.** So she must be shown to stay *exactly* where you've asked her to "Stand."

When she has become comfortable with this, add the next layer. This time when you ask her to "Stand," step back and walk to her hip, pause and go back to her halter, pause, then pick up the lead, make sure she sees you pick it up, say "Walk On" and go for a little walk again. Remember the figure eights.

Now switch sides and begin all over. Be careful to do everything slowly and methodically from the very first step of just walking and stopping in the figure eights.

When she's mastered both sides up to the point of your walking to her hip and back, it's time for the next layer. After you've asked her to "Stand," pause, then walk to her hip, and continue walking, to complete a circle around her, back to your starting place. Pick up your lead rope, congratulate her, pause, then walk on. Remember to ask her to "Walk On." Do this until she has it perfect, then switch sides. And that's it.

This whole exercise will take about half an hour to an hour. Of course over time she'll gain more and more confidence and you can try moving out of sight for a few seconds while she's ground tied, and then add more and more layers. Remember, if she moves, to ALWAYS put her back EXACTLY where she is asked to stand—never scold, always praise. It is also helpful to return to her BEFORE she moves—you want to celebrate the positive, not correct the negative.

One more tip, do not do this on grass until she has really learned to ground tie. It's not fair to tempt her.

Well there you have it. If you teach your horse this nifty little deal you can have a relaxed time at clinics, even if there you do hold the lead rope for safety, but your horse will not feel the need to fidget. She will stand relaxed, comfortable and confident. Tacking, grooming, trimming feet, everything will be soft, comfortable, safe and fun when your horse has the confidence to stand ground tied. She will thank you for teaching her.

Gitty Up ~ *Dutch Henry*

Get Out of the Way
and Let Your Horse Learn

Howdy Friends,

We've all been guilty of over-correcting our horses. We've all been guilty of demanding too much, too soon, too ... enthusiastically. Thank God, and the Spirit of the Horse, our horses have the patience to deal with us, our miscues, overstimulation, impatience and if I may risk saying so, our ignorance.

I understand training, trainers, lessons, competing and all the human things about horse and people relationships. And yes I understand the benefits and need for clear and consistent messaging, demeanor and posture. What I worry about is all the training, schooling and drilling tends to make us sometimes, and for some folks a lot of the time, overcorrect.

We've all seen people standing with their horse on lead, and when the horse dances and fidgets, the lead gets yanked and the person yells for the horse to "Stand Still!" The horse reacts, jerking its head high, stands still for a second, then dances again, then gets corrected in the same fashion again, and the correction follows again, and on and on it goes. And most likely this is the case every time that team goes away and stands together.

I submit yelling for the horse to "stand still" while tugging on the lead is what I call "overcorrecting." It short-circuits the learning curve, does not allow the horse to learn. And I'll wager it is not "consistent" with how that person normally carries themselves. Oh yes, it most likely IS consistent with how that person acts in that same situation, every time, and so the obliging horse is taught to dance, every time it is expected to "stand still."

So how do you fix that? Easy. Get out of the way, and let your horse learn to stand quietly with you, all day if that's what you want. Just do it. Simply stand still, don't over correct, in fact, don't correct at all. Choose to encourage instead. Sure, some horses are nervous, even scared sometimes, and are going to be high headed and fidgety by their nature. But how does barking at them or jerking the lead rope help reassure them? It can't. If we want them to feel safe and confident standing by us, we must exude safety and confidence, so they can mirror it.

It may take a number of weeks to accomplish this, especially if there are old habits, but simply standing with your horse, calmly and politely, on gravel or anywhere they won't be tempted by grass, hold the lead with your hand close to the halter at first, and just stand with her. Encourage her to be confident, self-aware. Allow her to look around, if she moves, politely put her back where you want her. Don't correct or say no. I like to use the word "stand." Not whoa. We are in fact standing, not whoaing. Just do it with smiles, happy and supportive, and after a while it'll be second nature for both of you.

I only used the "standing still with me" as an example, but there are many other times where we might be tempted to overcorrect or interfere with our horse's movement or expression. Ultimately, yes we have goals we want to achieve, things we want to do with our horses and we need to direct them, teach them, but try not always correcting. Try going with a mistake, see where it takes you. Follow your horse's spirit and not your blueprint. You can, and must, come back to your blueprint, but go with the flow, too. You will most certainly be given a gift.

Let me leave you with another example of not correcting and receiving a gift. I was in a spell when my back and legs were not good; those spells come and go, and in fact mess up my riding. Kessy and I were on the trail, it had been a while and even though we did our pre-ride exercises, she was a bit frisky and gaiting down the trail with glee, and some speed. She kept asking for the canter, finally I said, "Okay," and she went for it. I sit the canter, and feeling as I did that day, I couldn't keep my balance and in her attempt to stay under me she kept bouncing in and out of canter. I was laughing, and did give a slight tap on the rein to help her, but didn't correct her, I was just going to go with it and waiting for her to come back to her running walk. What she did was discover, to the surprise of both of us, she has a smooth and delightful ground covering rack! Before that moment neither of us knew it!

I wonder, had I corrected her, forced the canter, or the running walk, would we have discovered her awesome rack?

Of course there are times when correcting is necessary and is in fact the proper thing to do, but sometimes giving things a chance to work out on their own, perhaps blossom in ways we aren't even aware of, can be a priceless gift.

Gitty Up ~ *Dutch Henry*

Kessy Helps Us Find Her Fifth Gait!

◄─●──◄✲►──●─►

Howdy Folks,

On the 17th of this month (May 2013), Kessy and I will celebrate three years of our being a team. Over these 36 months, we've traveled many little journeys, enjoyed plenty of excitement, endured a few disappointments and had lots of fun and learning together. Yes, Kessy is a great student, and like all horses she is a great teacher, too. While I try to help her learn, she patiently, and sometimes not so patiently, teaches me too. We've enjoyed Coffee Clutch together nearly every morning. We've hit the trail 258 times for a total of 321 hours and if you figure 4 miles an hour, that's 1,288 miles. All those miles are barefoot miles. We've spent hours together in her "bedroom" writing stories. Kessy is half Tennessee Walker and half National Show Horse, which makes her one-quarter Arabian and one-quarter American Saddlebred. (Editor's note: On May 31, 2015, Kessy turns 12 years old, meaning she and Dutch have now been partners for five years.)

In our first months, she could not understand that standing still to mount at the mounting block was both correct and polite and also healthier for both of us. With patience and consistency, she learned to not only stand still to mount and dismount, but recently when this leg and left side of mine developed its silly issue, she learned to stand perfectly for me at the new mounting platform. My mounts and dismounts are not a thing of beauty, but her patience is.

Before coming to me, Kessy had never been on the trail, and of course never on the trail alone, which is how we always went, until recently. At first she would not go 100 yards down the trail. Thankfully at that time, mounting and dismounting was not so hard for me, and I'd get off and lead her. For a while I did a lot of leading.

Being Tennessee Walker, Kessy is a gaited horse, but at first she did not have the stamina, muscles or condition to maintain her stunning running walk for more than a few yards. I had felt it the first time I rode her, but as I say, only for a few strides.

In my opinion, the most important thing you can do to do to help a horse learn and develop the running walk is miles and miles and miles of "just plain walking." And we did that. We also practiced the exercises Diane Sept taught me, which are so very important to developing correct body posture and carriage, softness, off the forehand and never inverted. We also, with the help of Larry Wilson Saddles, made sure her saddle fit her "perfectly." Larry builds his own tree, right on the horse, tests the tree in motion, then puts the rest of the saddle together. He has made me three saddles over the years and they ALWAYS fit PERFECTLY.

Today Kessy can amble along in her "variable speed" running walk for miles, with the reins lying on the saddle, her head bobbing gently in time to the four-beat gait. Soft, smooth, powerful. Even with my not always so balanced posture, Kessy maintains her balance and stride.

So we were thrilled to learn that Kessy has four gaits—walk, running walk, trot and canter. Her canter is as smooth as any I've ever sat, and she "was" able to transition from running walk to canter without a hitch. Her smooth transition was possible, I believe, because she had become so balanced and self aware that she could simply maintain her posture and softly shift gears.

But then something happened. When my left side did whatever it did, I developed a problem sitting her canter. Her canter didn't change, Kessy didn't change—I did. My balance just goes away and Kessy has a hard time helping me find it in the canter. And yes, I do mean "helping me" … She'll try for her canter, I get all crooked, twisted and Kessy will begin to trot, change leads and even crowhop (very gently) trying to balance me. But I'm no help.

Then two weeks ago something really neat happened. I was trying to better my "canter seat" and Kessy was trying to "balance" me, in and out of canter and trot … All at once she balanced herself and me in a rack! WOW!! Soft, Smooth and quick! Kessy, where did that come from? A rack is a four-beat gait, like the running walk, but with shorter and quicker strides. It's delightful to sit and I was immediately balanced. And thrilled!

There is no doubt in my mind that all the miles of riding at a walk, developing her balance and her running walk, the saddle fit and the exercises, all made it possible for Kessy to find her rack. But holy cow this is too wonderful! In Kessy's attempt to carry me safely, at the speed I was asking for, she helped us discover her FIFTH GAIT … a smooth and stunning rack!

Now just as in the beginning with her running walk, she can only stay in the rack a short distance, but over the coming months, together we will learn this too. She needs to develop the muscles to maintain this new gait, and I need to "hear" what she is saying to help her. And Kessy, I am listening.

I share this story not only because Kessy and I think it's exciting but to encourage everyone to allow their horse the freedom and the time it takes to discover new things together. Because of all the things we did together the past three years, Kessy was determined to find a way to carry me, at the speed I asked for, in a way she could balance us both. I believe it is as simple, and glorious, as that.

Gitty Up ~ *Dutch Henry*

What Do You Do JUST For Your Horse?

Howdy Friends,

Yesterday I talked about Kessy and her willingness to find a way to keep both of us balanced at a quicker gait. It was that trying on her end that caused her to discover her newest gait, a rack. A rack is a four-beat gait, like the running walk, but with shorter and quicker strides. It's comparable to a quick trot in speed, and that's the story here. I'd been asking for a little more speed than the running walk, but I'd been having trouble sitting the canter lately, so Kessy had begun to drop in and out of canter, even mixing in a trot, while seeking balance, and she found a gait neither of us knew she had.

Why did she try so hard? I think she tried so hard because over the past three years we've developed a partnership. I don't mean a partnership where I'm the "boss" or "alpha horse." I know, we're all told we need to do that to gain our horse's respect and obedience. I've never bought into that. Don't know if I'm right or not, I just know that's not how I think. The partnership Kessy and I have is one of equals. Does she do everything I'd like? No … not yet. Do I do everything she'd like? No … not yet.

So how do you build a partnership of "equals" that works? I believe you've got to "give" to your horse. Most horse/human relationships are structured around "training." In one way or another, the human "trains" the horse to do what the human wants. Some folks say they're all about "natural horsemanship." I don't think there is anything "natural" about a round pen. But however they do it, the person expects their horse to be "trained" to the person's perspective. Some folks even say, "It's got to make sense to the horse." But often the training is still from the person's perspective.

Oh don't misunderstand me, training is necessary to the relationship, but if you work on the relationship first, the training is just more relationship building. What does that mean?

Sadly most horse/human relationships consist of feeding, training, riding, housing, grooming, hoof and other health care. All very important things indeed, but where is the horse's perspective in that? Sure they nicker when the person comes with the hay. Is it because she's happy to see the person, or the hay?

I believe for every hour spent in "training" at least as many hours should be spent "giving to the horse." Many horses are only in the ring with their person to be "worked" or "schooled" or "trained" or shown. The horse can't help but see the ring or round pen (or human) as anything other than a place of stress. Some horses will show it. Others will internalize it. The effects of that stress may not show up for years, but it'll show up. Then folks say, "I don't understand why he started being so ring sour," or slow, or lazy, or stubborn, or any of the many complaints we've all heard too often.

What if for every hour in the training session there was an hour spent in the ring just hanging out with the horse? A person could toss a flake of hay out and sit with their horse there and read a book, or work on their laptop, or just watch their horse relax and munch hay. Takes too much time? Actually it's good therapy for the human, too. And it's doing something for the horse, instead of expecting something from the horse. It's more powerful than simply turning the horse out in the pasture and going home. Because you're there with her, without asking for anything.

Doing the release and relax exercises, based on Linda Tellington-Jones' and Peggy Cummings' teachings, are a most wonderful way to "Do something just for the horse." These exercises "give to the horse" without asking or expecting anything of the horse. It's totally giving ... Total partnership building.

Sitting in the barn, or walking around their paddock, lot or pasture with them, just hanging out with them—this is partnership building. And in my opinion it is really important to the horse. Yes it does take time. But aren't they worth it? And I submit it is time very well spent for two big reasons. First, you'll actually need to spend less time training, because the relationship will be so strong. You'll hear your horse, and your horse will hear you. Cues are easier to hear, feel and follow for both horse and human. Second, these quiet moments do wonders for people too! We can all slow down a little.

I attribute Kessy's desire to try so very hard to take care of me that she found a new gait, a new way of moving, because she wanted to help her partner. Am I silly about that? Well, perhaps, but that's my belief ... And I suggest if you can find the time to just give to your horse, by offering the relax and release exercises, and just hanging out with her, be there "for her," without asking anything in return, your relationship will deepen in ways you can't imagine.

Gitty Up ~ *Dutch Henry*

Often a "Mouthy" Horse Has Some Other Issues

Howdy Friends,

A friend wrote and asked for advice about a "mouthy horse." … Figured I'd share what my thoughts are about horses who nip, pest and bother with their mouths. First and easiest, never, hand-feed a horse who is mouthy. Ever. Not even after you fix it. It's okay to give treats, carrots, apples and such, but drop them on the ground. Many mouthy horses became that way by hand feeding treats. It's not their fault.

Often a "mouthy" horse has some other issues—teeth, sore neck, sore feet, back or hips, just to toss out a few. She's only trying her best to tell you what's wrong. Often it is stress, just like a child who can't focus in school. Mouthy is fidget. She may be worried about the training you're going through and being mouthy is her way of fidgeting like a child in school. It may be her way of avoidance. She may have a difficult time focusing.

Her saddle may not fit. Sometimes they'll be mouthy or nippy when you try to catch them to tack up. Often this is mistaken for a lazy horse.

My best suggestion for mouthy horses and many other behavioral issues, is doing some or all of the "Therapy For Therapy Horses" exercises described in the earlier section of this book. I know I may sound like a one-note-band about those exercises, and I suppose I am … But they really work wonders. Be careful to do them in an area without grass, so the horse can focus. Do them ground tied or with someone holding a loose lead. Never discipline while doing these exercises. You'll see how quickly your horse will learn to ground tie. And focus.

I'm working with a young horse right now who was pushed too hard too young. He is very worried and stressed, and very mouthy. Even nippy. I see him once a week, just doing my exercises for 5 weeks now. We've made HUGE progress. His worry was that he'll be asked to do too much that he doesn't understand. The exercises just "Give To Him." They expect nothing of him. The first day I met him he was all over the place, and by golly those teeth could flash. Now already he ground ties and his mouthyness is better than 70% gone. And he never nips, which is a good thing since he is a therapy horse. Imagine if he could have had the exercises every day.

I do not recommend discipline for mouthy horses. Horses love to groom each other, and it's a sign of affection. They play games with each other, too. I feel, unless it is a safety thing, disciplining a mouthy horse confuses them and is a losing battle. Rather I suggest if you do at least the "Poll Wiggle," the "Neck and Vertebrae Wiggle," the "Belly Lift" and the "Rock Back" and more if you have time, every day for a few weeks, and simply ignore the mouthyness, you'll soon have a horse who can and will happily focus, and the mouthy thing will simply go away. Pay close attention as you do the exercises, especially the Vertebrae Wiggle, as she'll clearly tell you if you've found an "ouchy" area.

My mare Kessy was more than "mouthy" when we first teamed up. She had no reservations to outright biting. I employed these exercises along with my standard "Ignore the Negative & Celebrate the Positive" technique, as taught me by my mentor Diane Sept.

When a horse is mouthy, nippy or biting and we move to swat them, we usually miss. Part of it becomes a game for them, and in addition to what else may be bothering them, the new game is fun, and a sought-after distraction. If we don't miss, it does little to deter and a lot to chip away at trust. If we ignore it, they get no satisfaction, and eventually it simply goes away.

Hope you enjoyed this and will give a few exercises a try.

Gitty Up ~ *Dutch Henry*

Leader or Boss—For Your Horse

—————⟨✵⟩—————

Howdy Friends,

When I hear that tired old saw, "You need to show your horse who's boss," it gives me pause. I've never liked that approach any more than I like, "She's testing you, and you can't let her win" or "You need to be the 'alpha' mare."

"You need to be the boss," they'll say. Perhaps. But it's hard for me to wrap my head around the "boss" posture, when we really want to be partners.

Equals? I don't know, that one I can't answer. I do know there are plenty of days Kessy is more equal than me. I also ponder the advice that you shouldn't project "human emotions" onto your horse. Really? Maybe not, but I'd rather err along those lines than be the kind of person who thinks horses don't have emotions. Or can't feel them.

Leader instead of boss? Semantics, you say? I don't think so. I profess the words you think, and use, create your frame of mind and guide not only your conduct, but your emotions and attitude, and ultimately your actions as well. And don't we all agree that our horses are tuned into all of them? Remember my post awhile back about the power of the words we use for nicknames for our horses? Even if a horse owner thinks "Blockhead" is a cute name for their horse, you've got to admit it makes you feel different than when you say, "Handsome." Same goes for "leader" and "boss," I think.

Thinking from the boss' perspective, we might be more apt to demand rather than request. Correct rather than encourage. Even if it's a subconscious, innocent thing. I remember hanging on a fence one summer day watching a respected trainer give lessons. I remember too, how many times she called out to her student who was riding her lesson horse: "Make him turn," or "Make him stay on the rail." It was always "make him," never "ask him." That was a long time ago, but I never forgot it.

A boss perspective will have a controlling atmosphere rather than a guiding atmosphere. "Someone's gonna be in charge, either you or the horse," they'll say. Yet you read all over the place how you should build a partnership with your horse.

A "leading" perspective will create a true partnership. Leaders allow the time it takes to accomplish the mutual goals. They allow time for understanding. Leaders can see the missteps as baby steps along the way to achieving the goal. Leaders understand each member of the team shares equal benefits, and responsibility.

Leaders offer guidance, open the way, invite cooperation and lead by example. In my mind it's a wonderful thing to say, "You need to be your horse's leader."

Gitty Up ~ *Dutch Henry*

Gaited Horses and Saddles, Bits, Shoes and Stuff

Howdy Friends,

One of the many things I'm pretty fussy and outspoken about is saddle fit. Gaited horses are just that. Horses with multiple gaits. They walk, they trot, they have a flat walk, running walk, a rack and a canter. Some gaited breeds have even more gaits, like a fox trot. What they don't have is a need for a special saddle or equipment. They just need, as do all horses, a saddle that fits. If a saddle fits, it fits. Some gaited horses have high withers, others not so high. Just like other horses. Some are wide, some narrow. Just like other horses. Some have big shoulders, some don't. Some are tall and slab-sided, others are short and round, just like other horses. Why "experts" too often insist folks need "gaited horse saddles" is beyond me. Except as a selling tool for their saddles. And yes, I've seen the big name gaited horse saddles, and no, I've not been impressed. But I'm a simple fella. Either a saddle fits, or it doesn't. Simple.

What makes a saddle fit? A horse needs to be able to move under the saddle, while the saddle stays put. It's in the tree, or the flocking. Yup we need room at the withers, the shoulders, the spine. It can't be too long, too short, too wide or too narrow. It can't bridge, rock or pinch. It must be well balanced, can't lean forward or back, and certainly not to the side. But isn't that the case for all horses? If your saddle fits, a blanket will do, no pad required. It's not the saddle that gives a horse their gait—they're born with that. But an ill-fitting saddle can put a damper on gaiting if it inhibits any of the horse's moving parts.

But what about all those gaited horse bits? I ride bitless. Have for years, with many different horses. I use a little noseband hackamore. Discovered it in my endurance days. I love it, and every horse I've ridden has loved it. Often I've ridden in a halter only. (And no, I'm not a fan of the bitless bridles; the ones I've seen can put too much pressure on sensitive facial nerves.) I really got a kick out of the times I'd ride a horse for the first time and the owner hands me their bridle with a "walking horse" bit and I'd say, "I'll use this," showing my little rig. They always doubt it, then often say, "Wow, he never gaited like that for me!" It's not the bit that gives a horse their gait. They're born with it.

What about those special shoes? And I don't only mean only the horrible stacks and such they do to TWHs. There are the nasty plantation shoes and cog shoes and others, all causing damage to the foot, the joints, the legs and back. I ride barefoot. Have for a lot of years. Since before it was really catching on. And no long toes or high heels, either. A gaited horse's hooves should look just like any other hoof on any other horse. "He needs longer toes to gait," they say. "Hogwash!" I say. He needs healthy feet, just like any other horse. It's not the shoes or the trim that gives a horse their gait. They're born with it.

What about the other "stuff?" There are lots of gadgets, gimmicks and attachments out there some people insist are needed to "teach" a horse to gait. Many of them are too nasty for me to mention. Some not so nasty but equally unnecessary, and to some degree, harmful to the horse's biomechanics. It's not the stuff that gives a horse their gait. They're born with it.

An exciting note I'll share here. In my travels doing "Therapy For Therapy Horses" clinics, I have several times helped what folks call non-gaiting breed horses discover they could indeed gait. Arabian and Quarter horses to name the breeds. I wrote a fun blog post about one of those fun times, "Lilly's Surprise." And each time we had this experience, I only knew the horse a few hours, and their owner was riding in their regular tack, all I did was talk them through it.

So there you have it. A gaited horse is no different in what it needs than any other horse. They need love, respect, honor and a trusting rider who cares. Sit your horse, relax and say, "Gait please," and watch the world glide by.

Gitty Up ~ *Dutch Henry*

Lilly's Surprise

———⟨✦⟩———

Howdy Friends,

I noticed as she led Lilly, her footfalls and placement improved with almost every stride.

Lilly is a Quarter Horse. She's a beautiful 7-year-old black and white paint who loves her job working with children as a therapy horse. I had the honor of playing with Lilly and her teammates recently while conducting a Therapy For Therapy Horses clinic. Like all the horse partners there she receives the best of care. The owner and volunteers make sure it is a wonderful, fun and happy place for the children who come for healing, smiles and giggles, and for the horses too. And…they understand therapy horses need a little therapy too.

Our "Therapy For Therapy Horses" clinics are an all-day affair; the volunteers learn a lot of new things and the horses do too. The clinic is designed to teach and promote exercises that help the horse release, relax and maintain proper posture, and clear their minds. This was my second visit to this therapeutic riding center, so we added a few more fun exercises to the mix, and for me it was a delight to see what they'd learned a few months back had been incorporated into the routine care of all the therapy horses. As the owner says, "Without our horses we can't have equine assisted therapy, they are the heart of what we do."

"Lilly's surprise?" You might be asking.

Just as hard as the volunteers work to understand and master the techniques and exercises, so do the horses. It is honestly a lot to throw at them in just a day or two, so I'm careful to space out the layers of learning and allow for plenty of time for the horses to process the new feelings, releases and posture.

Near the end of the day, I noticed Lilly was a little overwhelmed. Her volunteer had worked hard to master the "one step" exercise, and while Lilly stood quietly after numerous repetitions, I noticed she was clearly asking for a break, so I asked a volunteer to simply lead her around the arena at a walk to help her relax and process. I thought they could just walk while I explained a bit more.

The other horses and volunteers stood quietly, and as I spoke I asked them to watch Lilly. This was a perfect opportunity to demonstrate how, while a horse might be cooperating and doing a great job, they might be internalizing confusion, stress or worry. I was hopeful by watching Lilly relax as she was quietly led that the volunteers would see the transition as she softened and lengthened. The reason I was pretty sure Lilly would be a good example is unless you looked really close it was hard to notice she needed a break. She's a very good girl.

I noticed as the volunteer led Lilly, her footfalls and placement improved with almost every stride. And I pointed out how she stepped perfectly heel to toe. How her hind feet came forward nicely to her front feet.

I asked for them to walk on a bit more quickly. Lilly began a soft half-a-hoof overstride with her hind feet under her and falling exactly on the track of her front foot. Her neck lengthened, her body lengthened and softened. In another lap Lilly had a full hoof overstride, and her carriage was beautiful, soft and rhythmic. I thought I knew what I was seeing and had to tease, "If I take Lilly home for a few months I'll bring you back a Quarter Horse with a running walk." We all laughed a bit as they kept up the pace.

I encouraged them to walk just a little faster as I explained a bit what was going on, then I turned to the owner and said, "Lilly's gonna get it right here, right now."

Everybody understood what we were trying for by now and they were having a grand time as we watched.

I instructed the volunteer to go just a little faster, keep Lilly at a walk, but move on just short of a trot. A few times Lilly did go to a trot, but the volunteer is really, really good, and soft, and she brought Lilly back to a brisk walk.

Then, on the third lap, Lilly stepped into a slow running walk! – WOW! – She could only hold it a few strides, but everyone saw it and burst into a cheer! It was soft and beautiful! Lilly got it two more times, just a few strides each time, but it was there and simply delightful.

Then we just knew we had to try it under saddle. And since this post is already long, I'll just tell you, after a few laps around, they got the slow running walk under saddle. Again just a few strides, but perfect and sweet.

Now to help Lilly build the muscles to maintain that sweet, soft running walk, they will ride her on the trail for miles and miles at a walk. And of course continue to do our release and relax exercises. Yes Lilly can and will still trot, canter and gallop, her new running walk is just another new gait she'll have. And folks, this was all done barefoot, on a loose rein, soft and easy. Simply beautiful!

Diane Sept often said she believed most horses can do a running walk and since this is not the first time with horses of other breeds I witnessed it, I sure believe it too!

What a wonderful surprise Lilly gave us, and I'm so tickled to have been there to be part of the fun!

Gitty Up ~ *Dutch Henry*

Get Out of the Way and Let Your Horse Gait—They're Born With It

※

Howdy Folks,

My Coffee Clutch post, "Gaited Horses and Saddles, Bits, Shoes and Stuff," generated some lively discussion, and a few questions. We had pretty much covered the fact that no special saddle, other than proper fit as with any horse, is needed. No special bit—in fact, no bit is needed. No special shoes; in fact, barefoot is best, for all horses, really, but that could be a subject for another blog day. You can read my thoughts on barefoot in my earlier post "Why Barefoot?"

I'll never forget the day I was riding along a beautiful "rails to trail" a number of years back, and a young woman rode toward us on a tall, stunning red and white paint. We stopped to chat, and as I'm wont to do, I looked the horse over as he danced and fidgeted beside us. I made note of the tight martingale, his shoes and high heels, his hollow back, thick inversion muscles and sad, worried eyes. The tack and saddle shined like a million bucks. Foam dripped from his mouth around I don't know what kind of bit. She held tightly on the reins, her legs jammed forward, as they had been when she rode toward me. I asked her what breed her beauty was. With a smirk she replied, "He's a registered, non-gaiting Tennessee Walking Horse." She must have seen the question in my eyes because she promptly added, "He's a registered Tennessee Walking Horse who we can't make gait. He's been to several trainers, and he just can't gait!"

I began to ask a question, but she cut me off. "Don't bother, I've heard it all. No one's ever gonna make him gait." With that she jerked him right, and trotted away.

"Make him gait." I've never forgotten that, obviously as I'm writing about it all these years later. I've never forgotten the look of that beautiful horse she rode either. All the signs, stress and breakdowns of a fine horse people were trying to "make gait." The over-collected, inverted, hollow backed look of a horse forced to gait, or try to, unnaturally.

Gaited horses will gait. They're born with it. All we need to do is **get out of their way and let them**. Simply sit your horse comfortably, in proper posture, as Sally Swift would say "in neutral," and allow your horse to walk on. After all, the flat walk and running walk are walks; they're just a little quicker.

The same muscles used to gait are the same muscles used to walk. Riding your horse for miles and miles and miles on the trail at a walk will develop those muscles, as well as a longer and longer soft and powerful stride. It is important that as you ride these miles at a walk, you allow your horse to relax, walk with their head down, off the forehand and on a loose rein. You know, get out of their way.

Trail miles are much preferred over riding in the arena, where no matter the size, your horse is always preparing to turn, and so are you. It's more difficult for her to "walk on" in the ring and develop her stride as she would during long continued muscle engagement on the trail. So really try for unending trail miles. Besides, it's better birdwatching on the trail, and more interesting for your horse.

In not too much time, you'll feel the stride begin to change; the hind end will become more powerful and engaged, and softer (and there are exercises you should consider to free up the hind end if your horse is short-strided). She'll begin to achieve a bigger overstride. All without forcing, over-collecting or gimmicks—or damage to her biomechanics. It'll be completely natural and make sense to your horse.

During this time it's fine to mix in a few canters, even trot if she wants to from time to time. What we are doing is building confidence in her long gait and her proper body carriage. And we are staying out of her way while she does it. I would say during this phase, look for at least 80% long, easy, but powerful walk.

When she tells you she's ready, find a nice long stretch of level trail, and ask her to walk faster. Be gentle and balanced and stay out of her way, but move her on and say, "Gait please." I use my right heel as a cue, and a lot of "kisses" and say the request over and over each time I tap my heel. She'll speed up instantly, and might try for a trot or pace. Using just one rein, tap her back, very gently, just short of the trot, at her fastest walk (pacing is not good for a horse, so don't do it). Then go right back to a loose rein and let her walk on a bit before asking again, congratulating her for the magnificent effort. Remember to smile.

Off and on, in safe level places along the trail ask for the "Gait please"—It'll come, just before the trot. If you did your walking miles loyally and politely, she'll give you her flat-walk or gait in just a few tries. Remember to praise her, and for every stride in gait say "Gait" so she learns the verbal request. At first she'll only hold her gait a few strides, and that's perfect. Keep helping her build those muscles. It takes a few months to build up the power to sustain it, but really, it's just this easy. She'll learn the verbal cue fast too.

Her head should be level, with her withers and back, her stride soft and long, her head will bob a little, and you'll feel the glide. In time together, you'll develop a variable-speed running walk. Just stay out of her way, and enjoy the ride.

Gitty Up ~ *Dutch Henry*

Saddle Pitch and Inverted Hips

———⟨✦⟩———

Howdy Friends,

Recently I've had conversations with a few folks who were experiencing tripping, stumbling and other things such as horses appearing distant, unwilling or sore. Each had different descriptions of what was happening and all had been given, as we might expect, a wide variety of courses of action to correct the "problems." Of course, each case could be examined separately, and a wide variety of human-related things can be the cause of horses tripping, forging, being sore, uninterested, etc.

We talk often of the importance of "saddle fit." Unfortunately saddle fit is, and always will be a challenging endeavor. And in many cases costly too. But they are our horses, entrusted to our care, and few things are as important as a correctly fitting saddle. I'm often surprised at the money folks are willing to spend on all sorts of horse-related items, including trucks and trailers, and of course buying a horse, but are so reluctant to spend the money it takes to get the most important piece of tack perfect.

In saddle fit we all know about room over the withers, sort of. We all know about clearance for the spine, sort of. Some folks know about rocking and bridging. Many folks know about tracing the withers so they get the tree width correct, sort of. Many know about proper flocking, and the proper length of a saddle. What about saddle pitching?

I had the opportunity to see the photo of one of the folks whose horse was tripping, sitting her horse. As the photo opened, I noted the posture of the rider's head and shoulders, not bad, but slightly off. The horse carried its head low; the rider had a firm hold on the reins, and her legs were tight, and her pelvis tilted forward. The saddle pitched ever so slightly downhill, forward. Admittedly it was just a photo snapped for fun, and none of us are ever posed as we would like to be. However, it was clear in this case, the unlevel saddle caused the inverted posture of the rider, and this would be a constant in that saddle, or any saddle that pitches unlevel.

The tipping forward saddle will not only hurt the horse but makes it impossible for a rider to find their neutral seat. That is, the rider's pelvis will tip toward the front, inverting (hollowing) her spine and causing her to ride inverted. As the body tries to compensate, she has no choice but to put too much pressure into the stirrups, and that transfers negative energy through her body and the horse's. The rider's inverted posture will cause the horse to go inverted, causing trips, stumbles, loss of focus, soreness and breakdown.

You can learn a lot about the "neutral" position from the books of Peggy Cummings and Sally Swift.

Can you shim a saddle to make it level? Yes, however that should be a temporary fix. Shims all have edges, possibly causing pressure points, and they can move. It only takes five pounds of pressure per square inch to stop the blood flow to the capillaries in a horse's back.

How can you check to see if your saddle is level? With your horse standing square, and level, let your eyes trace over the seat. From a few feet back, standing at the side, look softly at the seat from back to front. You'll notice if it is pitched forward if you look for the imaginary line running through the center of the seat, be it English or western. If a western-type saddle, the cantle and horn can confuse you, so it's best to look at the seat.

Unlevel saddles can be the cause of a lot of problems for rider and horse. If when riding you feel as if you need to use your legs too much to sit comfortably, if you think you are having a difficult time finding your neutral seat, your saddle is most likely pitching. It will invert your hips. Your inverted posture will cause your horse to become inverted, and that is really bad for both of you.

Gitty Up ~ *Dutch Henry*

Suddenly—Don't Use in Writing or Horsemanship

Howdy Folks,

I often think about, and write about, how living and working, or playing and learning with our horses, and writing have so many similarities. Such as my blog, "Horses and Writing Similar POVs?" and "Building Confidence in a Horse and Building a Character in a Novel." Another time I wrote about "It's About Who They Are, Not What They Are"—one of my favorites.

The other day I was reading a writer's blog about the overuse of the word "suddenly" in a manuscript. Every word she said was exactly correct, and I'd hoped she would say more. I've always found the word "suddenly" to be a speed bump in a story or novel. Instead of propelling me forward with the action as the writer intends, it stops me dead in my reading tracks. Pushes me away. In fact most "ly" words have that effect on me. If the author replaces the "ly" word with the action she's trying to portray, we readers can be drawn in and feel the action. Instead of "hearing" about it. But "suddenly" for me is the worst of the "ly" words.

Here's a brief example. "Suddenly she burst into tears." Not much there, even if we knew why she had to cry. How about something like, "She needed to see him again. Where was he? Why can't she find him? Sucking short breaths, she tried to be strong, but her burning eyes flooded, tears streamed down her face."

I've always found while I'm editing, if I re-write scenes or sentences replacing "ly" words, the scene embraces me more. Adds depth, meaning and emotions. Yes it will add words, but I suggest they are words that build emotions and connection with the reader. And for writers, aren't they the two most important things?

In our relationship with our horses, "emotions and connection" are most important as well. If we do anything "suddenly," it's more than a speed bump to our horse. It's a "failure to communicate." And as "authors" of the moment, it's our job to "re-write the scene."

If we replace that "ly" word, or action, with a more descriptive series of words and actions, our horse will follow us, feel the emotion, and sense the connection. And our relationship will deepen.

It makes no sense to the horse when we bark commands, jerk on the lead rope or wave our hands and arms. Sure, we get a reaction, and that's just what it is, a reaction. It's not a connection. It's best, even if the horse is making a mistake, to follow through that mistake, see where it takes you, then build on it. Write the scene with easy to embrace description.

Engage your imagination, your intuitiveness, let your horse help write the scene in a way that embraces both of you. It'll add words, but those words make all the difference.

Gitty Up ~ *Dutch Henry*

Why Do We Focus On Training?

◦──◦⟨✦⟩◦──◦

Howdy Friends,

Training, and trainers, are of course important. To be fair, many things must be taught, and learned, by both horse and person. Training is the backbone of so many disciplines folks pursue with their horses, from trail riding, western pleasure, showing, hunter-jumper, dressage, and on and on. Sure we need to learn what we're doing. We and our horse, and that requires lessons, and training. Sometimes plenty of both.

I've heard it said that every time you're on your horse, you should be training. That's an interesting paradigm. I don't intend to take anything away from the importance, or benefits, of training. But every time you're on your horse?

Over the years I've met folks who take lessons and go to clinics all the time. I've met folks who do nothing else in between. They just go to clinics and take lessons. They may not ride for weeks, sometimes months at a time. Some folks board their horses at training barns, and only ride when it's time for the next lesson. And for them, that's perfect ... But what if it could be more perfect?

I suggest folks can establish much deeper relationships with their horses by not always focusing on training. Mix in plenty of just being together time. For sure, not everyone can start their day like I do, having coffee in the barn with their horse. A lot of folks don't have the luxury of having their horses at home. If that's your case, be sure you spend time with your horse other than just showing up for lessons and training. They'll love you for it. Learn a few exercises you can do on the ground, even in the stall with your horse, to help their posture and body carriage.

I believe all horses should have plenty of easy going, "don't think about nothin'," trail time. Just go down the trail, do some chatting with friends, or better yet, go alone. Just you and your horse. Don't forget to watch the birds! The training will simply fall into place if you don't focus on it all the time. Just let it happen. Allowing yourself and your horse to work through mistakes in an unstructured moment is rewarding. Let the mistakes happen and see where they lead you. Enjoy your horse so she can enjoy you. And remember, find time for that relaxing trail time.

Gitty Up ~ *Dutch Henry*

They Taught Me Patience

Howdy Friends,

"They taught me patience." That's what about thirty percent of the respondents answered to a recent month's TrailBLAZER magazine's Facebook question, "How have horses changed your life and made you a better person?"

While there were many diverse and touching answers folks shared to that question, a few brought tears to my eyes, "They taught me patience," was the overwhelming number one response. If we add to that number the folks who said things like their horses taught them to look inside themselves, take time to enjoy the day and slow down to understand, that number would rise considerably.

It is interesting to note so many could learn that simple and very important life lesson from their horses. But it tells us more. It tells us what high quality teachers horses truly are. By their nature, horses are patient, ever willing to endure our impatience until we learn to slow down and hear them. Then they are there for us, ready to guide us into the realm of simple understanding.

Patience and horses – to some those two can't go together. Especially today in our every busy, impatient world. To those folks I'd like to suggest, give it a try. Expect nothing except that you allow your horse to move into your spirit, touch your heart and guide you to a place where you can truly see the world's magnificence, and the beauty and wisdom of your teacher. When we find true patience and harmony within ourselves, things are accomplished in less time. And to a higher refinement.

Gitty Up ~ *Dutch Henry*

Celebrate the Positive
Ignore the Negative

Howdy Folks,

When I talk about Kessy having been such a biter when we first met and I'm asked how I fixed it, I always answer, "Celebrate the positive and ignore the negative." Kessy had serious trust and friendship issues when we first met, and if I stepped into her bubble I was sure to get snaked—you know, the pinned ears, stretched out threatening neck and flashing pearly whites. If that didn't work she'd turn those pearly whites into bites. And by golly she was fast! Yup, she bit me a number of times, only twice badly, but there were lots of little bites those first 6 or 10 months.

So how do you ignore all that? Sometimes it's not easy, but unless it is truly dangerous—and two times she did get disciplined with eyeball to eyeball, voice raised, glaring, sneering, yes the end of the world is coming, mean nasty explaining, followed immediately by a hug and reassurance—you must ignore it.

Just as with children and some adults, I believe this sort of behavior is a call for attention. In horses, it can also be a sign of misunderstanding, disobedience, dominance, illness, poorly fitting tack, poor cues or a host of other possible triggers. And to discipline might not only be exactly the wrong approach, it will chip away at any confidence and trust they might have, or are trying to build.

Ignoring it will get you much further. If you can adopt the standard of ignoring the negative and celebrating the positive most all the negatives simply go away.

Discipline then becomes a rare thing indeed. If our desire is to build a true partnership, we don't want a worried, compliant horse; we want a robust, full spirited and trusting horse for a teammate who understands they can make a mistake, just as we do, and not be disciplined. They'll also know they get love and praise and will be celebrated for the positive they do.

It follows then, and it really does, that they will stop doing the negative things because there is simply no reward or gain, and will do many more positive things for the rewards of praise, love and connection.

As I have written before, it was six months before I could hug Kessy. When we first met she did not even want to be brushed. I've worked with other horses over the years with these and other issues and always, "Celebrating the positive and ignoring the negative" has healed them and strengthened them in marvelous ways—while disciplining could never have done anything more than create a compliant horse.

There is a whole other world of this most wonderful technique, if she is never disciplined for making a mistake, she will be more willing to try new things, and get them correct sooner. She'll have the eagerness and confidence to really try without worry of being corrected for every misstep.

I believe it's a pretty darn good philosophy in life too. There is plenty of negative out there, but we don't need to give it credence. If our first instinct becomes to ignore the negative, the positives can find us more easily, and isn't that a whole bunch better? I promise if you adopt this standard you'll see your horse in a new and shining light, and a whole lot of other things, too.

Gitty Up ~ *Dutch Henry*

Our Dreams and Memories of Horses Who Have Crossed the Rainbow Bridge

Howdy Friends,

Our thoughts of our departed equine partners, I believe, are a connection to their spirits. Not merely memories, though memories are precious, but conduits by which we travel and visit with them again and again.

How often have we slept comfortably and been visited by long ago, physically gone friends in dreams so real we could feel them, smell them, hear them? Friends who in days past had carried us gleefully across fields, trails and on adventures? Friends who stood silently with us and joined us in celebrating our joys. Helped shoulder the burden of our disappointments, our sorrows. The spirit of the horse can be so tightly woven into ours that it is highly appropriate it would continue to lift us after they have left the physical realm, continue to guide us, comfort us, lighten our hearts.

On a sunny day, busy with whatever task we'd undertaken, a sudden wisp of a thought brings a departed partner back with a nicker and a snort. Perhaps a headshake and stomping foot. Perhaps an invisible muzzle touches our cheek.

While riding our present horse, a thought of how to cue, move or sit dashes into our head and we think, "There you go old friend. Thanks for the help." They talk to us still, ever present, helpful and connected.

Here's a picture of my dear Diablo some years back. One of the finest horses I've ever had the honor of learning from.

My old friend Diablo, while never less than a high-spirited boy, has dropped in often to reassure, even guide my thoughts over the years. Funny how he mostly appears when I'm troubled. But then he always was at his best when I needed the most help. I believe it was his wisdom that helped me see, my spirit guides are horses.

While Honey was only with me a short time, she too connects from time to time, in her quiet, unassuming way. She was never less than a perfect gentlelady.

Often I get thoughts from/of horses I barely knew, perhaps worked with, but the images and thoughts are clear and sometimes deep. I believe when a connection has been made, the conversation continues forever. If we listen, they will talk.

Friends, if you have those sudden thoughts, peaceful dreams and ideas that seem to come from nowhere, embrace them. They are your friends visiting.

Gitty Up ~ *Dutch Henry*

Dear sweet Honey,
she loved the trail and helping me write stories!

SECTION VII

Those Who Shaped Me

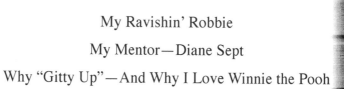

My Ravishin' Robbie

Howdy Folks,

Without my Ravishin' Robbie, what would life be?

Yesterday as I enjoyed my Coffee Clutch with Kessy, Saturday, the cats, the chickens and wild birds, the train let go its lonesome whistle. Birds sang in the treetops their glorious, happy tunes, calling in the struggling spring. Knowing our forecast was for yet another blast of cold and a bit of a wintery mix, I figured they knew it already and were making the most of this spring-like day. My mind drifted to my Ravishin' Robbie. She'd been gone four days and was coming home this evening, but I missed her so.

Some fellas do just fine when their sweeties are away. I'm not one of them. Married thirty-nine marvelous years, I remember our first date. I remember her yellow dress. Boy howdy she always looks great in yellow. We weren't on a date with each other, it was a double date and she was with the other fella. But by golly I knew I needed to get to know her better. Even if she did kinda boss me that night. That hasn't changed much over the years. I reckon that's why God matched us up; he knew I'd be a better man with her love keeping me straight.

Some folks say they married their best friend. Yea I figure I sure did that, and so much more. We've traveled through some mighty big adventures together, some great and some not so great, but always as a team. We had the indescribable joy of raising a fabulous daughter, who blessed us with our sweet grandbabies.

I'd had a pretty rough start on life, and had never known the feeling of love before I met Robbie. What she saw in this collection of oddities that is me, I'll never know. But I can still remember the feeling I got way back then on that first date, just being with her; that life made sense now. I still have that feeling, with her I'm complete. I always say, "Everything good I learned about life, I learned from my wife."

Thank you God, for introducing us. Thank you, Ravishin' Robbie, for puttin' up with me.

If you look at the top left of our Coffee Clutch blog page where I describe what I write about, you'll notice love is in there. I know what Robbie has given me is the deepest kind of love.

Gitty Up ~ *Dutch Henry*

My Mentor—Diane Sept

Howdy Friends,

I could not have ended this book without introducing you to my mentor, Diane Sept.

For more than 40 years, with a kind heart and a keen sense of human/horse communication, Diane has, in her very special, gentle way, helped people learn to connect with and understand their horses. There is something quite unique in the way she can help folks "hear" and understand their horses.

If you've been following my Coffee Clutch blog or my Facebook, page you've heard me mention Diane more than a few times. You might have even seen me saying, "Whatever good I know about life I learned from my wife, and whatever good I learned about horses I learned from Diane Sept." I had the privilege and honor of working with and learning from this exceptionally talented and caring horse person for nearly ten years and under her tutelage helped rehabilitate ex-show Tennessee Walking Horses.

From simply having a pasture buddy, to trail riding, endurance riding, showing, dressage or anything in between and beyond, Diane teaches her students that everything is important. I truly believe Diane may well be the first "holistic" riding instructor/ horse trainer. She certainly was on the forefront of addressing the biomechanics, nutrition and natural health of both the horse and rider.

Diane was a barefoot advocate long before the current movement was gathering its present momentum. She is a huge advocate of the natural health and well being of horses. She doesn't simply "train" a horse or "teach" a student. Rather she considers the entire relationship between student and horse and helps to fine tune all aspects. Being a long time student and believer of Linda Tellington-Jones, she employs Tellington TTouch® techniques to be certain the horse is free to move in the manner required to perform what is being asked. She teaches if we listen to the horse, and take care of her health, body, posture, balance, confidence and self-carriage, all things can be accomplished without gadgets, devices or gimmicks in a truly natural way.

As one of Peggy Cummings' original certified Connected Riding® Instructors, Diane has been teaching Connected Riding for over 20 years and is a Certified Senior Instructor. Diane has performed for national Centered Riding symposiums and Connected Riding demonstrations. She has even been known to give bridleless and gaited dressage riding demonstrations at various venues. While she specializes in gaited horses, she welcomes all breeds. Freeing up and allowing the natural abilities of any breed to express themselves is one of the goals of Diane and Connected Riding.

Diane's commitment to the betterment of horses' health everywhere is what sets her apart. She is not only a trainer and instructor—she is a true Horse Advocate. As one of the original members of Friends of Sound Horses (FOSH) and judge from the onset, she has been decrying the horrible act of soring and other abuses of the Tennessee Walking Horse and other gaited breeds for decades. She has helped to make a difference. But she does not limit her efforts to gaited breeds and is a defender of horses' rights to be pain free, no matter the breed.

Through her gentle instruction, her students learn to achieve levels of accomplishments, connection and understanding with their horses, and themselves, that they may have never imagined possible. She teaches the student it is not only the physical act of learning a technique, but the whole of the experience. The best and healthiest result for both horse and human.

Diane is pure in her intentions, and it comes through in her actions and words. She has touched and changed countless lives, both horse and human. I know, I'm one whose life was made richer for knowing her and will be forever grateful for what she has taught me. It is because of her I am able to do my "Therapy For Therapy Horses" clinics, so from afar, Diane is helping horses help people.

Thank you Diane for all you do to help so many. And thank you Connie Bloss for introducing me to Diane all those years ago.

Gitty Up ~ *Dutch Henry*

Why "Gitty Up"
And Why I Love Winnie the Pooh

Howdy Friends,

Winnie The Pooh held my hand in my darkest moments.

From time to time, I am asked about my love for Winnie The Pooh and my signature, "Gitty Up."

We became friends in those years when as a young boy I'd been locked in a room for three years, before they put me out on the farm and I found the spirit of the horse. Horrible things happened in that room, things that continue to haunt me today. But at some time in those room-years, I somehow got a Winnie the Pooh book. I used to pretend that room, with its solitary window painted black, was the Hundred Acre Wood. Like Pooh, Piglett, Tigger, Kanga, Roo, Eyore and Christopher Robin, my adventures in the Hundred Acre Wood were imaginary, but Pooh was a terrific imaginary guide.

Pooh Bear has been a steady and loyal friend throughout my life, always ready with a funny story or song, and advice. I credit him with my love of honey. And butterflies.

My email signature comes from Pooh Bear. Our daughter, the sweet and terrific Abbie, had a Winnie the Pooh desk calendar a few years ago and on July 17 that year Pooh was dressed as a cowboy and the caption was, "Gitty Up Pooh Bear." She sent it to me with a note, "Thought you would like this." That little picture and her note resides on the table under glass by my chair ever since. About that time I was just beginning to find my way around a keyboard. I noticed folks had clever and heartfelt sign offs at their siggys. So I latched on to "Gitty Up, Dutch Henry," and except for the most formal emails, that's what I use.

I often wonder what folks think about that. But just as the spirit of the horse has in fact saved my life, so too did a tiny, yellowish brown, inquisitive, funny and heroic bear hold my hand in the darkest moments.

I think I'll shovel an extra spoon of honey on my oatmeal this morning.

Gitty Up ~ *Dutch Henry*

RESOURCES & REFERENCES

Diane Sept
Back to Basics Equine Awareness
clinics, lessons and seminars
www.dianesept.com

Peggy Cummings
Connected Riding and Groundwork books
DVDs, clinics and seminars
www.connectedriding.com

Linda Tellington-Jones
Tellington TTouch
books, DVDs, clinics and seminars
www.ttouch.com

For more from Joe Camp
on what's in it for the horse:
www.thesoulofahorse.com

Jaime Jackson
Barefoot hoof care and natural care for horses
information, books, DVDs, tools
& the "Paddock Paradise" book and info
www.star-ridge.com

Pete Ramey
Barefoot hoof care, books and DVDs
www.hoofrehab.com

TrailBLAZER Magazine
www.trailblazermagazine.us

Natural Horse Magazine
www.naturalhorse.com

Yvonne Weltz
"The Horse's Hoof" newsletter
www.thehorseshoof.com

Spencer LaFlure
Whole Horse Dentistry
www.advancedwholehorsedentistry.com

Will Falconer, DVM
Homeopathic veterinarian
www.vitalanimal.com

Joseph Thomas, PhD
Chinese herbalist
www.forloveofthehorse.com

SOURCE ® micronutrients for animals and people
Seaweed based micronutrients
to aid all metabolic process
www.4source.com

Dutch Henry
is available for motivational speaking

As one can see by the stories in this book,
Dutch's philosophy for a happy, productive and
successful life is to focus on the positive.

"Ignore the negative and celebrate the positive"
is Dutch's guidepost. Whether your focus
is on managing a company, building loving
relationships with family and friends, or simply
finding a way to see the beauty and splendor of
every day, every moment, Dutch Henry can help
you understand that it's easy to be happy with
yourself.

To engage Dutch Henry for your events,
meetings, workshops and functions,
email him at dutchhenry@hughes.net

ABOUT THE AUTHOR

Dutch Henry is a horse advocate, freelance writer and novelist who lives in central Virginia with Robbie, his wife of 39 years, along with one horse and a number of dogs, cats and chickens. He writes about "People & Horses Helping Horses & People" and has columns in trailBLAZER and Natural Horse magazines. His stories tell of the people and horses who give so much to help others. He has also had articles featured in numerous other equine magazines. He is active on Facebook and his Coffee Clutch blog where he writes about horses, birds and nature, the art of writing and, of course, his Coffee Clutch where he begins each day having coffee with his mare Kessy and critters gathered 'round. He enjoys spending time with his wife along with trail riding, bird watching, nature walking and interviewing the wonderful people about whom he writes. He also does free "Therapy for Therapy Horses" clinics at equine assisted therapy centers and equine rescues.